P9-DIA-190

COMPACT *Research*

Nuclear Weapons and Security

by Lauri S. Friedman

Current Issues

ReferencePoint Press™

San Diego, CA

For more information, contact
ReferencePoint Press, Inc.
PO Box 27779
San Diego, CA 92198
www.ReferencePointPress.com

Picture credits: Maury Aaseng, 35–38, 54–57, 73–74, 89–92
AP/Wide World Photos, 9, 17

Series design:
Tamia Dowlatabadi

LIBRARY OF CONGRESS CATALOGING-IN-PUBLICATION DATA

Friedman, Lauri S.
  Nuclear weapons and security / by Lauri S. Friedman.
    p. cm.— (Compact research series)
  Includes bibliographical references and index.
  ISBN-13: 978-1-60152-021-0 (hardback)
  ISBN-10: 1-60152-021-2 (hardback)
  1. Nuclear weapons. 2. Terrorism. I. Title.
  U264.F73 2008
  355.02′17—dc22
                                                                    2007016581

Contents

Foreword

As modern civilization continues to evolve, its ability to create, store, distribute, and access information expands exponentially. The explosion of information from all media continues to increase at a phenomenal rate. By 2020 some experts predict the worldwide information base will double every 73 days. While access to diverse sources of information and perspectives is paramount to any democratic society, information alone cannot help people gain knowledge and understanding. Information must be organized and presented clearly and succinctly in order to be understood. The challenge in the digital age becomes not the creation of information, but how best to sort, organize, enhance, and present information.

ReferencePoint Press developed the *Compact Research* series with this challenge of the information age in mind. More than any other subject area today, researching current events can yield vast, diverse, and unqualified information that can be intimidating and overwhelming for even the most advanced and motivated researcher. The *Compact Research* series offers a compact, relevant, intelligent, and conveniently organized collection of information covering a variety of current and controversial topics ranging from illegal immigration to marijuana.

The series focuses on three types of information: objective single-author narratives, opinion-based primary source quotations, and facts and statistics. The clearly written objective narratives provide context and reliable background information. Primary source quotes are carefully selected and cited, exposing the reader to differing points of view. And facts and statistics sections aid the reader in evaluating perspectives. Presenting these key types of information creates a richer, more balanced learning experience.

For better understanding and convenience, the series enhances information by organizing it into narrower topics and adding design features that make it easy for a reader to identify desired content. For example, in *Compact Research: Illegal Immigration*, a chapter covering the economic impact of illegal immigration has an objective narrative explaining the various ways the economy is impacted, a balanced section of numerous primary source quotes on the topic, followed by facts and full-color illustrations to encourage evaluation of contrasting perspectives.

The ancient Roman philosopher Lucius Annaeus Seneca wrote, "It is quality rather than quantity that matters." More than just a collection of content, the *Compact Research* series is simply committed to creating, finding, organizing, and presenting the most relevant and appropriate amount of information on a current topic in a user-friendly style that invites, intrigues, and fosters understanding.

Nuclear Weapons and Security at a Glance

Nuclear Powers

Nine nations have nuclear weapons: the United States, Russia, France, China, the United Kingdom, India, Pakistan, Israel, and North Korea.

Active Nuclear Weapons

About 27,000 active nuclear weapons exist worldwide, with 95 percent belonging to the United States and Russia.

The United States Arsenal

The United States has 9,962 nuclear weapons stationed in locations within the United States and around the world. This includes 5,735 active or operational warheads: 5,235 strategic; 500 nonstrategic.

Highly Enriched Uranium

Highly enriched uranium (HEU) is one substance that makes a nuclear weapon so powerful. HEU is derived from the element uranium, which contains a naturally occurring isotope known as U-235. Uranium must undergo extensive processing to enrich the amount of U-235 to at least 90 percent to become weapons grade.

The Nuclear Non-Proliferation Treaty (NPT)

The NPT allows the United States, Russia, France, China, and the United Kingdom to legally own nuclear weapons. It prohibits these nations from helping others attain nuclear weapons and prohibits nonnuclear-weapons states from attaining nuclear weapons. Nearly 190 nations have ratified the treaty as of 2007.

India and Pakistan

India and Pakistan did not sign the Nuclear Non-Proliferation Treaty. They developed nuclear weapons in 1974 and 1998, respectively, but have never used nuclear weapons in the multiple wars they have fought against each other.

Iran

Although Iran claims to be pursuing nuclear technology for peaceful purposes such as electrical power, it is widely believed to be working on nuclear weapons projects. Much of the world wants at all costs to prevent Iran, which has established ties to terrorist groups, from acquiring nuclear weapons. U.S. intelligence predicts Iran will make its own nuclear weapon in 10 years.

Israel

Although Israel has neither confirmed nor denied it possesses nuclear weapons, the United States believes it developed nuclear weapons in 1979. It is believed to have made its bombs using highly enriched uranium that was stolen from a U.S. recycling plant in the 1950s and 1960s.

North Korea

North Korea is the only nation to have ever withdrawn from the NPT and developed nuclear weapons. On October 9, 2006, it tested its first nuclear bomb. It is believed to possess enough highly enriched uranium to make between six and ten small nuclear weapons.

Use

The United States is the only country to have ever used nuclear weapons in wartime, when it dropped atomic bombs on the Japanese cities of Hiroshima and Nagasaki at the end of World War II.

Nuclear Winter

Earth's climate could be severely altered by explosions using less than 0.1 percent of the world's nuclear weapons. Scientists estimate that on average, the temperature of Earth's surface would drop by about 2.25°F (1.25°C), plunging all continents into climate upheaval that would lead to severe famine and drought.

Overview

Overview

❝ The bomb is back, and nuclear dangers are on the rise again, not only in North Korea but around the world. ❞

> —David Cortright, research fellow at the Joan B. Kroc Institute for International Peace Studies at the University of Notre Dame.

❝ All of the evidence indicates that the threat of nuclear, biological, or chemical war has diminished to a lower level than at anytime in most of our lifetimes. ❞

> —William M. Arkin, military analyst for NBC News and the *Washington Post*.

Nuclear weapons are the most dangerous weapons on the planet. They have this reputation for good reason: Nuclear weapons are capable of killing thousands, even millions, in mere minutes; completely obliterating buildings in an entire city; and leaving behind dangerous radiation that can render an area unlivable for decades. But what exactly is a nuclear weapon? Why were they invented, and why do countries continue to build them? Answering these and other questions is critical to determining whether the nuclear weapons problem is becoming worse or improving.

What Is a Nuclear Weapon?

Nuclear weapons are made terrifically powerful by the inclusion of one of two materials: highly enriched uranium (HEU) or plutonium. Both of these are highly unstable substances that require extensive, complicated

This image shows the devastation left after the United States dropped an atomic bomb on Hiroshima, Japan, in August 1945.

processing to become what is called "weapons grade." HEU is derived from the element uranium, which contains a naturally occurring isotope known as U-235. Natural uranium is only about 0.7 percent U-235. But through extensive processing, the amount of U-235 in the uranium can be increased to 20 percent or more. The greater the concentration of U-235, the more powerful the weapon. Weapons-grade HEU developed by the military is usually enriched to 90 percent or more, but less-enriched uranium can still be used to create a crude nuclear device. With regard to stolen fissile materials, officials tend to be more concerned about HEU than plutonium, because the use of plutonium in a nuclear device requires more technical knowledge, resources, and infrastructure than HEU.

> " The ... bomb dropped on Hiroshima ... was small by modern standards, about 15 kilotons. In comparison, the United States' combined arsenal is estimated to be about 1,800 megatons, an amount that, if detonated, could destroy life on the entire planet. "

Nuclear weapons come in several different sizes. They range from 10 to 550 kilotons and larger. The atomic bomb dropped on Hiroshima, Japan, which ended World War II, was small by modern standards, about 15 kilotons. In comparison, the United States' combined arsenal is estimated to be about 1,800 megatons, an amount that, if detonated, could destroy life on the entire planet. Furthermore, since the atomic bomb was dropped on Japan, more powerful nuclear weapons have been developed. As of 2007, about 27,000 active nuclear weapons exist in the world, and enough HEU and plutonium exist to make about 240,000 more. It is estimated that as much as 1,900 tons of HEU is stockpiled around the globe, and more is produced every year to power civilian infrastructure such as nuclear power plants and submarines.

Why Were Nuclear Weapons Invented?

Nuclear weapons were invented by the U.S. Army Corps of Engineers during World War II. Some of America's most famous scientists, including Albert Einstein and J. Robert Oppenheimer, were involved in the development of the atom bomb. Their work was carried out under the Manhattan Project, a four-year effort that succeeded in developing three nuclear weapons. One, code-named "Little Boy," was detonated over Hiroshima on August 6, 1945. Another, code-named "Fat Man," was detonated over another Japanese city, Nagasaki, on August 9, 1945. These remain the only times any country has ever used a nuclear weapon against another country in a war.

More than 200,000 people died from the bombings, and Japan immediately surrendered to the United States and its allies. In addition to ending the war, the United States showcased its possession of the most dangerous weapon the world had ever seen, immediately establishing itself as a superpower in a new world order. Its possession of nuclear weapons was threatening to nations such as the Soviet Union, which was wary of U.S. power. To counter the influence of the Americans, the Soviets began pursuing the bomb, and in 1949, after a combination of scientific research and espionage, the Soviets successfully tested a nuclear weapon that was the same size and strength of the Fat Man bomb dropped on Nagasaki. The nuclear arms race had begun.

The two superpowers began a weapons buildup the likes of which had never been seen. In addition to increasing their own supplies, each nation helped their allies develop nuclear weapons. In this way, the United Kingdom got the bomb in 1952; France shortly followed in 1960. Communist China, an ally of the Soviets, acquired nuclear weapons in 1964. Slowly, the globe became dotted with nuclear-weapons nations, and more countries fervently worked so they too could have access to the cutting-edge technology.

Curbing the Spread of the Most Deadly Weapon

Seeing the potential for global devastation if nuclear weapons were to become too prolific, the world's superpowers agreed in 1968 to limit the number of countries legally allowed to own nuclear weapons. Called the Nuclear Non-Proliferation Treaty (NPT), the agreement (which officially came into force in 1970) allows the five states that had weapons prior to the treaty to retain their arsenals. It prevents these states from assisting any other state from developing nuclear weapons and prohibits nonnuclear-weapons states from ever developing them. "Considering the devastation that would be visited upon all mankind by a nuclear war," the treaty states, "[we] have agreed as follows: each nuclear-weapon State Party to the Treaty undertakes not to transfer to any recipient whatsoever nuclear weapons or other nuclear explosive devices. . . . Each non-nuclear-weapon State Party

> " Seeing the potential for global devastation if nuclear weapons were to become too prolific, the world's superpowers agreed in 1968 to limit the number of countries legally allowed to own nuclear weapons. "

to the Treaty undertakes not . . . to seek or receive any assistance in the manufacture of nuclear weapons or other nuclear explosive devices."[1]

The NPT was an important first step in curbing the spread of nuclear weapons, but not all nations were willing to be limited by it. In 1974, for example, Indian scientists developed nuclear weapons. India had not signed the NPT; neither had Pakistan, which developed the bomb in 1998, bringing the two longstanding enemies dangerously close to the brink of nuclear war. During this time another nation is believed to have developed nuclear weapons. Though Israel has never admitted to having nuclear weapons, it is thought to have become a nuclear power in 1979.

An Effective Tool Against Nuclear Weapons Proliferation?

Although the NPT did not prevent these nations from acquiring nuclear weapons, it has succeeded in both preventing countries from starting nuclear weapons programs and convincing those with programs to abandon them. In the early 1990s, for example, South Africa, which possessed six nuclear weapons, dismantled them in accordance with the NPT; Belarus, Kazakhstan, and Ukraine, each of which held Soviet nuclear weapons, similarly relinquished nuclear stocks on their soil, giving them to Russia in the 1990s. Argentina, Australia, Brazil, Egypt, Japan, Libya, Spain, and many other nations have abandoned their pursuit of nuclear weapons in accordance with the treaty they have signed.

For these gains, the NPT has been hailed as "a key legal barrier against the spread of nuclear weapons" by Stephen G. Rademaker, assistant secretary of state for arms control. As Rademaker said to the United Nations on the NPT's anniversary, "That we can meet today, 35 years after the Treaty entered into force, and not count 20 or more nuclear weapons states—as some predicted in the 1960s—is a sign of the Treaty's success."[2] Indeed, as of 2007 nearly 190 nations have

> **As of 2007 nearly 190 nations have signed the NPT, indicating a truly joint effort to curb the spread of the world's most dangerous weapons.**

signed the NPT, indicating a truly joint effort to curb the spread of the world's most dangerous weapons.

Yet others see the NPT as an inadequate and ineffective way of preventing nuclear-weapons states. Writes law professor Liaquat Ali Khan, "The NPT is poised to fall apart in the near future . . . [because it] can be lawfully dumped."[3] Indeed, in 2003 North Korea withdrew from the treaty and, to the dismay of most of the international community, in 2006 successfully tested its first nuclear weapon. As one author said of that development, "The notion of nuclear weapons in the hands of a 'crazy state' frightens people."[4] Another called it "the most serious threat to [U.S.] national security."[5]

> **One of the most ironic facets of nuclear weapons is that they are desired precisely to prevent their use.**

With the number of nuclear powers now at 9, about 40 others are suspected to have enough nuclear materials to either quickly build bombs or to get nuclear weapons programs up and running. One such nation is Iran, a signatory of the NPT and a nation believed to have ties to terrorists. Turkey, Syria, and Saudi Arabia and the Gulf Cooperation Council, which consists of the nations Qatar, the United Arab Emirates, Bahrain, Kuwait, and Oman, are also believed to be working on nuclear weapons programs, which would violate the NPT as well.

Why Do Nations Want Nuclear Weapons?

One of the most ironic facets of nuclear weapons is that they are desired precisely to prevent their use. Indeed, most nations desire nuclear weapons for the sole purpose of deterring another nation from attacking them. It is widely understood that if a nuclear nation were to be hit, it would retaliate using the most powerful weapon in its arsenal and devastate the attacking country. When both nations have nuclear weapons, this too prevents their use, because if they were to attack each other, both would likely end up destroyed. This defensive strategy is called Mutual Assured Destruction (MAD), and for years kept the United States and the USSR at a nuclear standstill. If either power ever used their nuclear weapons on each other, they would both end up obliterated, and thus the threat of MAD continually prevented nuclear war.

The Cold War has long ended, however, and some nations today that seek nuclear weapons do so to prevent more powerful countries from intervening in their affairs. For example, this is the case with Iran, which has long been at odds with the United States and the international community over its desire to acquire nuclear technology. The United States considers Iran to be part of an "axis of evil" that should under no circumstances have access to nuclear weapons. Indeed, Iran has given support to terrorist groups in the past and thus is not considered a trustworthy holder of such powerful devices.

Yet from Iran's point of view, it wants nuclear weapons to ensure its survival. Iran is currently surrounded on all sides by countries that host large numbers of U.S. troops, and the United States has made it clear it is hostile toward the ruling Iranian regime, which wants, like all sovereign nations, to avoid being overthrown. As American Foreign Policy Council vice president Ilan Berman puts it, "Iranian policymakers have embraced the idea of nuclear weapons as central to ensuring regime stability, and to 'preempting' the possibility of military action on the part of the United States."[6] As a sovereign government, some believe Iran has the right to do this. "To be sure, the United States and its allies have reasons to be bothered about Iran's behavior," says former U.S. ambassador to NATO (North Atlantic Treaty Organization) Robert E. Hunter, "but Iran also has reason to be concerned about its security."[7]

The War in Iraq: Curbing or Boosting the Desire for Nuclear Weapons?

Interestingly, the March 2003 invasion of Iraq that was intended to prevent former dictator Saddam Hussein from developing weapons of mass destruction likely encouraged rather than discouraged Iran from pursuing its nuclear program. Iranian leaders likely saw Hussein's lack of nuclear weapons as a critical weakness that allowed him to be overthrown. Political science professor Stephen Zunes explains:

> Iraq, which had given up its nuclear program over a decade earlier and subsequently allowed IAEA [International Atomic Energy Agency] inspectors back in the country

to verify the absence of such a program, was invaded and occupied by the United States. By contrast, North Korea—which reneged on its agreement and has apparently resumed production of nuclear weapons—has not been invaded. The Iranians may see a lesson in that."[8]

Indeed, many believe that the Iraq war has served not as a warning for states to abandon their aspirations of developing weapons of mass destruction but as a reason to hasten their programs in order to protect themselves against invaders. As Khan has written,

> U.S. foreign policy has created a global context in which it is far more protective for states to have nuclear weapons than not to have them. The war on Iraq demonstrates that a state without weapons of mass destruction is vulnerable to invasion and occupation. It would be perfectly logical to conclude that Iraq was attacked not because it had weapons of mass destruction but because it had none.[9]

Indeed, the War in Iraq likely spurred certain nations already at odds with the United States to take all steps to preserve their security.

A Tool for Blackmail

Another reason nations seek nuclear weapons is to have leverage in negotiations. This is a driving desire behind North Korea's nuclear weapons program. The North Korean people live in severe hardship under the brutal dictatorship of Kim Jong Il. Kim's commitment to communism and militarism has isolated North Korea from much of the world, depriving that country of trading partners and the ability to provide basic substances such as food, fuel, and medicine for itself.

> " Many believe that the Iraq war has served not as a warning for states to put aside their aspirations of developing weapons of mass destruction but as a reason to hasten their programs in order to protect themselves against invaders. "

Thus, North Korea's strategy has been to develop nuclear weapons in order to blackmail the international community into giving it much-needed aid. Indeed, North Korean leaders have turned the threat of building nuclear weapons into billions of dollars and millions of tons of food from donor nations since the mid-1990s. The North Korean "regime's survival depends on blackmailing foreign countries into giving it the food and fuel that it cannot produce for itself,"[10] writes journalist Gwynne Dyer.

> "Indeed, North Korean leaders have turned the threat of building nuclear weapons into billions of dollars and millions of tons of food from donor nations since the mid-1990s."

In one example of such blackmail, in 2002 when approximately a million North Koreans starved from famine and flood, North Korea restarted its nuclear program and specifically let U.S. officials know about it, hoping to get them to drop sanctions against them and allow North Korea to receive food, fuel, and medicine. When the United States did not remove the sanctions, North Korea moved forward with its program, seeking the weapon it could use to get the international community to oblige it.

Indeed, when Kim Jong Il finally built a nuclear weapon in 2006, many experts interpreted it as playing the final card in a decades-long blackmail game. Whether he will successfully blackmail the international community into supporting his country remains to be seen. Immediately following the North Korean nuclear test, the United Nations reaffirmed sanctions against the nation in a move that some saw as ineffective, believing it is better to simply give the North Korean leader what he wants to avert a nuclear crisis. Writes Dyer, "Like any professional blackmailer, . . . Kim would probably relinquish his nuclear weapons if he were offered enough food and oil aid, an end to trade embargoes, and a firm United States promise not to try to overthrow him. None of that would cost very much, and the United States is not going to attack him anyway."[11] Yet others, such as foreign policy expert Aaron L. Friedberg, believe that giving into Kim's demands will only worsen the problem. "Responding to Kim's recent actions by showering him with rewards and respect will secure his reign and leave him free to continue accumulating fissile material," he says. "Such a policy will also do irreparable damage to what remains of the nonproliferation regime and send precisely the wrong message to Iran's mullahs [leaders], who are watching our every move with intense interest."[12]

A Matter of National Pride

Finally, nations want nuclear weapons as a matter of pride. To be a part of the nuclear club is to attain great status and authority. Indeed, the five nations that are allowed by the NPT to own nuclear weapons are the only permanent members of the UN National Security Council and thus exert power over every other nation in the world. Operating a successful nuclear weapons program also implies technological and scientific superiority, international acceptance, national sovereignty or independence,

This image, from 1996, shows North Korea's spent nuclear fuel rods in a cooling pond. Recent activity at the power plant, picked up by spy satellites, has become a concern to the United States and South Korea.

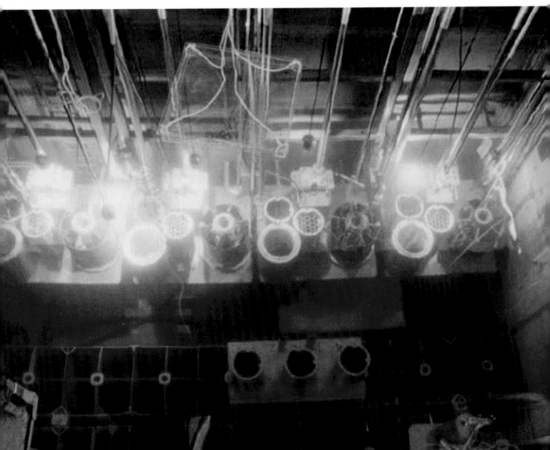

> **Nations will continue to pursue nuclear weapons programs . . . to prove their technological and scientific superiority and to flex the independence they are supposedly accorded as a sovereign nation.**

and clout. Cato Institute analyst Ted Galen Carpenter sums up this attraction in a single word: "Prestige. The global nuclear weapons club is a very exclusive organization. . . . Countries that have nuclear weapons are treated differently than are non-nuclear powers."[13]

Furthermore, the nuclear world of "haves" and "have-nots" established by the NPT is very difficult for most prideful nations to swallow. Simply put, Iran and other nonnuclear nations do not like the idea that other nations should tell them what to do. There is an inherent elitism in allowing certain nations to have nuclear weapons but not others. Zunes has recognized this elitism as "a kind of nuclear apartheid," arguing that "not only are such double standards unethical, they are simply unworkable: any effort by America to impose a hierarchy of haves and have-nots . . . simply fuel[s] rebellion from the have-nots."[14] Nations will continue to pursue nuclear weapons programs, in other words, to prove their technological and scientific superiority and to flex the independence they are supposedly accorded as a sovereign nation.

Making Good on a Devastating Promise

Interestingly, the decades of nuclear de-escalation efforts that Western nations, particularly the United States, have pursued in order to reduce or weaken nuclear supplies for the good of the planet may prove to be their Achilles heel when it comes to preventing rogue nations from acquiring nuclear weapons. The United States may have the largest nuclear arsenal in the world, but decades of downsizing and apologizing for the use of atomic bombs at the end of World War II have caused some to worry that rogue nations may no longer believe the United States would actually use its weapons to attack. As one journalist writes, nuclear weapons "owners have thankfully rendered it [the threat of nuclear war] irrelevant by disuse, but in doing so have deprived it of deterrent effect. Britain's bomb did not deter Argentina from invading the Falkland [Islands in 1982], nor was America's massive arsenal a deterrent in Vietnam, Lebanon, Somalia or Iraq."[15]

Indeed, most associate the dropping of a nuclear weapon with insane, short-sighted recklessness, and this is precisely the threat that the untrustworthy regimes leading Iran and North Korea pose. In other words, leaders of those nations may just be irresponsible enough to use such weapons. U.S. leaders would probably not undertake the decision to use nuclear weapons lightly; but some believe that in order to be effective the United States must remind the world it is willing to wield the awful power it possesses in order to protect itself and its allies.

Living in a Nuclear World

In 1963 President John F. Kennedy said, "I am haunted by the feeling that by 1970, unless we are successful, there may be 10 nuclear powers instead of 4, and by 1975, 15 or 20. . . . I see the possibility in the 1970s of the President of the United States having to face a world in which 15 or 20 or 25 nations may have these weapons."[16] Kennedy's worst fears did not materialize; in the year 2007 just nine nations are nuclear powers, and scores of others have abandoned their weapons programs or relinquished weapons they already had. From this, many deduce that nuclear proliferation is a serious yet stabilized issue that does not seriously threaten Americans or anyone else. As military analyst William M. Arkin has said, "All of the evidence indicates that the threat of nuclear, biological, or chemical war has diminished to a lower level than at anytime in most of our lifetimes."[17]

> " Just nine nations are nuclear powers, and scores of others have abandoned their weapons programs or relinquished weapons they already had. From this, many deduce that nuclear proliferation is a serious yet stabilized issue that does not seriously threaten Americans or anyone else. "

But others see the growing ambitions of terrorist groups, the amount of unsecured nuclear weapons and materials, and the addition of North Korea to the nuclear club as troubling developments that signal the problem of nuclear proliferation is worse than it has ever been. According to political science professor David Cortright, the world has entered "an era in which the nuclear danger has become more diffuse and unpredictable. . . . The risk of a bomb actually exploding in a city somewhere is arguably greater now than during the Cold War and is likely to grow in the years ahead."[18]

> **The world has lived with nuclear weapons since the end of World War II with no incident and can continue to do so provided that everyone in the world shares an interest in preventing their use.**

Regardless of whether the problem has improved or worsened overall, nuclear nations may be just what the United States and its allies must live with. The international community has few options for preventing nations from acquiring nuclear weapons, and none of those options are foolproof. It may be that acknowledging the reality of nuclear weapons proliferation is a most effective step in developing strategies that will best reduce the chance of nuclear war. Writes columnist William Langewiesche, "It is important to recognize that the spread of nuclear weapons is a condition over which we do not have control and for which there is no solution. . . . Pretending otherwise, or imagining that we can impose order when we lack the power to do so, is the surest recipe for self-destruction and disaster."[19] Indeed, the world has lived with nuclear weapons since the end of World War II with no incident and can continue to do so provided that everyone in the world shares an interest in preventing their use. "Perhaps," concludes journalist Simon Jenkins, "learning to live with nuclear power, in all its forms, will be the great challenge of the 21st century."[20]

Is the United States Likely to Be Attacked with Nuclear Weapons?

> **Our offensive against nuclear terrorism should have the highest priority. It should be equipped with all the leverage we can provide it. That's not the case today. And that's why the experts can confidently say: It's only a matter of time.**

—James E. Goodby, former U.S. ambassador.

> **Could terrorists really obtain sufficient materials and put together all of what would be needed to manufacture a nuclear weapon? I'll go out on a limb and say, not after 9/11.**

—William M. Arkin, military analyst for NBC News and the *Washington Post*.

The threat from nuclear weapons is taken very seriously in both the political and scientific communities, and everyone agrees that a nuclear terrorist attack would dwarf the attacks of September 11 in horror and scope. Yet whether terrorists would be able to acquire or build their own nuclear weapons is a matter of continuous debate.

The Nuclear Ambitions of Terrorists

Most experts agree that if terrorists were able to get their hands on nuclear weapons, they would not hesitate to use them against the United States or its allies. It seems clear that terrorists would want to launch a nuclear attack if they could; terrorists increasingly seek to destroy as many lives as they can in as dramatic a spectacle as possible. Indeed, al Qaeda leader Osama bin Laden has repeatedly called for the mass slaughter of Americans, saying, "I swear to God that America will not live in peace."[21] Sulaiman Abu Ghaith, Osama bin Laden's press spokesman, has claimed that al Qaeda intends "to kill 4 million Americans including 1 million children."[22] The only weapon capable of such devastation is a nuclear weapon.

Some of America's top officials have confirmed al Qaeda's interest in obtaining nuclear weapons. George Tenet, director of the Central Intelligence Agency until 2004, testified before Congress that "Al-Qaeda's interest in chemical, biological, radiological, and nuclear weapons is strong. Acquiring these is a religious obligation in Bin Laden's eyes. Al-Qaeda and more than two dozen other terrorist groups are pursuing these materials. . . . For this reason we take very seriously the threat of a chemical, biological, or radiological attack."[23] In another round of testimony, navy veteran Patrick Briley claimed to have seen transcripts from interviews with captured al Qaeda members that reveal "al-Qaeda is targeting nine U.S. cities with the highest Jewish populations for attack with suitcase nukes and/or multiple dirty and toxic plutonium type radiological weapons."[24]

Could Terrorists Make Their Own Nuclear Weapon?

Despite the fact that terrorists want nuclear and other weapons of mass destruction, it remains unclear whether they would actually be able to acquire them. Terrorists would have three options for acquiring nuclear weapons: to build them on their own or to buy or steal them from nuclear-enabled nations.

Most experts agree that terrorists lack the infrastructure, materials, brainpower, and financing to build their own nuclear weapon. Terrorists would need to make the key ingredient of a nuclear bomb, highly enriched uranium (HEU) or plutonium. Yet it takes a very high level of scientific skill to make these materials and would also require large facilities, such as processing plants, that can usually be built only by very large and wealthy companies or governments.

Even if terrorists had such facilities, they would likely be detected by organizations such as the International Atomic Energy Agency that patrol the globe searching for unauthorized nuclear weapons factories, and also by space programs such as NUDET, the Nuclear Detonation Detection System, a U.S.-owned space-based system that detects, locates, and reports on nuclear explosions in Earth's atmosphere and near space. NUDET acts like a bomb alarm to let authorities know if weapons are being tested, which is illegal under international law. Nuclear proliferation expert and former assistant secretary of defense for policy and plans Graham Allison has repeatedly stated, "Terrorists could . . . attempt to create new [nuclear] supplies, but doing so would require large facilities, which would be visible and vulnerable to attack."[25] Therefore, because they would neither have the resources to make nuclear weapons materials nor would these resources likely escape detection if they did have them, it is not probable that terrorists would be able to make their own nuclear weapon. As one group of authors writing in the *Bulletin of the Atomic Scientists* noted, "Terrorist-produced fissile material is so extremely unlikely that it's safe to call it impossible."[26]

Would a Nuclear Nation Sell Terrorists a Nuclear Weapon?

More possible is that terrorists could acquire existing weapons or the materials for weapons from countries in the nuclear club. Indeed, there are nations with nuclear technologies, such as Iran and North Korea, that have made clear their desire to see destruction brought to Israel, the United States, and other Western nations. When North Korea successfully tested a nuclear weapon in October 2006 and became the ninth nation to possess nuclear weapons, the immediate worry of politicians, scientists, and citizens was that they would sell their technology to the highest terrorist bidder.

Some fear that the rogue governments at the helm of these nations would indeed be willing to cooperate with terrorists to fulfill their dream of destroying the West. Iran, for example,

> " When North Korea . . . became the ninth nation to possess nuclear weapons, the immediate worry of politicians, scientists, and citizens was that they would sell their technology to the highest terrorist bidder. "

has long been suspected of having ties to the terrorist group Hizballah and other terrorist groups active in Iraq. Iran commonly refers to the United States as the "Great Satan" and has made no secret its desire to see the United States and its allies, especially Israel, fall from power.

North Korea, too, might consider selling its weapons to terrorists. The internationally isolated nation suffers from severe financial problems and might consider selling nuclear technology as a way to reap extra income. Indeed, terrorists seeking nuclear weapons have enormous coffers—Osama bin Laden alone is a billionaire. Financially strapped governments could be tempted by such financial incentives. "Rogue regimes in Iran and North Korea are moving ever closer to developing nuclear weapons that will surely find their way into the hands of terrorists," writes one editorialist.[27]

Jealously Guarding Their Arsenals

Others, however, believe it is unlikely that a nation would willingly give nuclear weapons or materials to terrorists. First, nuclear regimes would have little incentive (other than financial) to give such closely guarded technology away—after all, it makes them vulnerable to a nuclear attack themselves, should relations with the terrorist group sour. Second, nations that might be inclined to sell nuclear technology to terrorists do not have very much of it—it is estimated that North Korea has only enough enriched plutonium to make a handful of small, weak bombs. Nations that have poured so much money, time, and pride into their national nuclear programs would likely be unwilling to share it with terrorists at any price. Ted Galen Carpenter, a leader of defense and foreign policy studies at the Cato Institute, has pointed out that Iran has never sold terrorists other weapons of mass destruction it possesses. "Why," he asks, "should one assume that the mullahs [Iranian leaders] would be more reckless with nuclear weapons when the prospect of devastating retaliation for an

> **Nations that have poured so much money, time, and pride into their national nuclear programs would likely be unwilling to share it with terrorists at any price.**

attack would be even more likely? The more logical conclusion is that Iran, like other nuclear powers, would jealously guard its arsenal."[28]

Undeniably, if terrorists did obtain this material to use against the United States, the result would be devastating. But once the United States determined who sold the terrorists their weapons, it is certain that the United States would retaliate, possibly with its full arsenal of nuclear weapons. Such an attack on the offending nation would be so crippling, its survival would be highly doubtful. As reporter William Langewiesche has written, "We can make it emphatically clear that if we or our most important friends are ever hit by terrorists with a ready-made nuclear device, we will immediately devastate whatever regime is to blame."[29] Therefore, in the interest of self-preservation, even nations with hostile intentions have thus far been deterred from selling or giving their nuclear secrets to terrorists.

> " In the interest of self-preservation, even nations with hostile intentions have thus far been deterred from selling or giving their nuclear secrets to terrorists. "

Could Terrorists Steal a Nuclear Weapon?

Even though most nations would probably not give terrorists nuclear technology, terrorists might be able to steal nuclear secrets from nations with poorly guarded nuclear industries. From some perspectives, the chance of nuclear weapons being stolen has been drastically reduced by the number of nuclear nonproliferation actions taken since the end of the Cold War. Indeed, both the United States and Russia have retired thousands of nuclear weapons from service, removed nuclear weapons from aircraft and naval vessels, and amended protocols that dangerously kept nuclear weapons on the brink of being launched. The United States and Russia are not the only nations that have taken measures to secure or reduce their arsenals; the United Kingdom, France, and China have either reduced or not added to their nuclear arsenals. According to military commentator William M. Arkin, "Worldwide stockpiles of nuclear weapons have declined by more than two-thirds since the late-1960's Cold War peak."[30] Fewer available

> **Even if a nuclear weapon could be stolen, it would likely be equipped with safety features that would prevent a thief from detonating it.**

nuclear stockpiles means fewer for terrorists to steal from.

Furthermore, international efforts have succeeded in getting Libya, South Africa, Brazil, Argentina, Japan, Sweden, and other nations to relinquish their nuclear programs; nuclear-weapons-free zones have been established in Latin America, the South Pacific, Africa, Southeast Asia; and efforts continue to establish one in the Middle East. Each of these efforts has prevented more nuclear weapons from entering the global market. Finally, even if a nuclear weapon could be stolen, it would likely be equipped with safety features that would prevent a thief from detonating it. Russian nukes need to be detonated using hard-to-come-by access codes, for example, while Pakistani nuclear weapons are reportedly stored separately from their active cores.

Under Constant Threat of Theft

Yet evidence abounds that nuclear weapons and materials can and will be stolen. "Almost every month, someone somewhere is apprehended trying to smuggle or steal nuclear materials or weapons,"[31] says Allison. It is estimated that more than half of the former Soviet nuclear arsenal remains unsecured and even unaccounted for. Furthermore, some worry that scientists of the former Soviet Union and other nations will sell their skills to terrorists out of a need either for income or prestige. Evidence of this was brought to light in 2004 when Abdul Qadeer Khan, the father of Pakistan's nuclear weapons program, confessed to heading a clandestine international network of nuclear-weapons-technology proliferation in which he shared Pakistan's nuclear secrets with Libya, Iran, and North Korea. Said John R. Bolton, undersecretary for arms control and international security, of this development: "It is clear that the recently revealed proliferation network of A.Q. Khan has done great damage to the global nonproliferation regime and poses a threat to the security of all states."[32] Indeed, many attribute North Korea's acquisition of nuclear weapons to the nefarious efforts of the A.Q. Khan network.

Even nuclear materials that are used for civilian purposes could provide an opportunity for terrorists to steal what they need to make a nuclear weapon. Civilian utilities, such as nuclear power plants, nuclear-powered submarines, and nuclear-powered icebreakers (used to break up ice in remote regions such as Siberia) run on small amounts of highly enriched uranium, the material that gives nuclear weapons their devastating power. Indeed, around 20 interceptions of stolen fissile material have been recorded from such sources. One incident occurred in August 2004, when a Russian nuclear technician named Alexander Tyulyakov was arrested for trying to steal HEU used in Russian submarines and icebreakers. Another occurred in 2007, when a smuggler was caught in the Republic of Georgia trying to sell stolen HEU.

To prevent civilian HEU from being stolen and sold to terrorists, authorities have argued that HEU should be discontinued in civilian endeavors. Advises Center for Nonproliferation Studies analyst Cristina Chuen, "Moving towards the elimination of the civilian use of this material is an important part of the fight against WMD [weapons of mass destruction] terrorism, since HEU is the terrorist's fissile material of choice for constructing a nuclear device."[33]

> " A 2005 survey of more than 80 nuclear proliferation experts concluded that the risk of terrorists acquiring stolen fissile material constitutes the greatest threat to American security. "

The Race to Prevent an Attack

Whether stolen from civilian or military activities, authorities remain concerned that a nuclear attack using stolen HEU is imminent. Indeed, a 2005 survey of more than 80 nuclear proliferation experts concluded that the risk of terrorists acquiring stolen fissile material constitutes the greatest threat to American security. In the survey, which included the opinions of senators Sam Nunn and Richard G. Lugar, General Norman Schwarzkopf, CIA director James Woolsey, former defense secretary William Cohen, and former weapons inspector David Kay, experts determined there is a 70 percent chance of a nuclear terrorist attack using fissile material acquired on the black market being carried out in the next 10 years.

But the experts are also quick to point out that the United States and the international community still have time to take steps to prevent the worst from happening. "There has not been," as of 2007, "any documented theft of enough fissile material for a crude nuke,"[34] and the United States has committed $1 billion annually to be spent on the Nunn-Lugar Cooperative Threat Reduction Program, which is leading international efforts to secure nuclear weapons and materials around the globe. The race to prevent terrorists from acquiring nuclear weapons and materials is sure to continue throughout the 21st century and hopefully, combined with other nuclear proliferation prevention efforts, will be successful in preventing a nuclear terrorist attack.

Is the United States Likely to Be Attacked with Nuclear Weapons?

66 I was close enough to the real dangers of the Cold War that the risk of a nuclear war never seemed academic to me. But I have never, I have never been as worried as I am now that a nuclear bomb will be detonated in an American city. I fear that we are racing towards an unprecedented catastrophe. 99

—William Perry, "Post–Cold War U. S. Nuclear Strategy: A Search for Technical and Policy Common Ground," remarks to the National Academy of Sciences, August 11, 2004.

Perry was the secretary of defense under President Bill Clinton.

66 The probability of a terrorist attack with an actual nuclear weapon cannot be reliably estimated, and it is surely lower than the probability of virtually any other type of terrorist attack. 99

—Veronique de Rugy, "Is Port Security Spending Making Us Safer?" working paper #115, American Enterprise Institute, September 7, 2005.

De Rugy is an adjunct scholar at the Cato Institute. Her research interests include tax competition, financial privacy, bioterrorism, and fiscal sovereignty issues.

Bracketed quotes indicate conflicting positions.

* Editor's Note: While the definition of a primary source can be narrowly or broadly defined, for the purposes of Compact Research, a primary source consists of: 1) results of original research presented by an organization or researcher; 2) eyewitness accounts of events, personal experience, or work experience; 3) first-person editorials offering pundits' opinions; 4) government officials presenting political plans and/or policies; 5) representatives of organizations presenting testimony or policy.

66 There are currently some 1,900 tons of HEU stockpiled around the globe while more is produced every year. As the material of choice for would-be nuclear terrorists, it is critical that everything that can be done to secure, consolidate, reduce, and ultimately eliminate this material is done as quickly as possible. 99

—Cristina Chuen, "Reducing the Risk of Nuclear Terrorism: Decreasing the Availability of HEU," Center for Nonproliferation Studies, May 6, 2005.

Chuen is an analyst at the Center for Nonproliferation Studies, an organization that makes recommendations on how to curb the spread of nuclear weapons.

66 The risk of a bomb actually exploding in a city somewhere is arguably greater now than during the Cold War and is likely to grow in the years ahead. 99

—David Cortright, "The New Nuclear Danger: A Strategy of Selective Coercion Is Fundamentally Flawed," *America*, December 11, 2006.

Cortright is president of the Fourth Freedom Forum in Goshen, Indiana, and a research fellow at the Joan B. Kroc Institute for International Peace Studies at the University of Notre Dame.

66 All of the evidence indicates that the threat of nuclear, biological, or chemical war has diminished to a lower level than at anytime in most of our lifetimes. 99

—William M. Arkin, "The Continuing Misuses of Fear," *Bulletin of the Atomic Scientists,* September/October 2006.

Arkin is the author of *The Alternative: Terrorism, Weapons of Mass Destruction, and the American Future.*

❝All of today's great powers share an interest in the proposed campaign [to prevent terrorists from acquiring nuclear weapons]. Each has sufficient reasons to fear nuclear weapons in terrorists' hands, whether they are al Qaeda, Chechens, or Chinese separatists.❞

—Graham Allison, "How to Stop Nuclear Terror," *Foreign Affairs*, January/February 2004.

Allison is a former assistant secretary of defense for policy and plans under President Bill Clinton and currently teaches at Harvard's Kennedy School of Government.

❝Not only do nuclear thieves stand a chance in Russia (and elsewhere), they have repeatedly been successful, stealing weapons-usable nuclear material without setting off any alarm or detector.❞

—Matthew Bunn and Anthony Weir, "The Seven Myths of Nuclear Terrorism," *Current History*, April 2005.

Bunn and Weir work for the Project on Managing the Atom in the Belfer Center for Science and International Affairs at Harvard University's John F. Kennedy School of Government. They research nuclear theft and terrorism, nuclear proliferation and measures to control it, and the future of nuclear energy and its fuel cycle.

❝Nuclear terrorism is not easy. . . . There are no known cases of theft or purchase of an intact nuclear weapon, so a terrorist attack with one is more than unlikely. There has not been any documented theft of enough fissile material for a crude nuke—although there have been attempts.❞

—Linda Rothstein, Catherine Auer, and Jonas Siegel, "Rethinking Doomsday," *Bulletin of the Atomic Scientists*, November/December 2004.

Rothstein is the editor of the *Bulletin of the Atomic Scientists*.

66We need an aggressive U.S. policy aimed at denying terrorists the pool of nuclear weapons and related materials from which they can buy or steal the means to destroy an American city. . . . It should dry up the most serious potential sources of nuclear terror; the weapons that are stockpiled, the new weapons that are being built, and the infrastructure that supports these programs—and not just in Russia.99

—James Goodby, "U.S. Must Take Offensive Against Nuclear Terrorism," *Baltimore Sun,* February 4, 2007.

Goodby is a former U.S. ambassador and the author of *At the Borderline of Armageddon: How American Presidents Managed the Atom Bomb.*

66Intelligence reporting indicates that nearly 40 terrorist organizations, insurgencies, or cults have used, possessed, or expressed an interest in chemical, biological, radiological, or nuclear agents or weapons.99

—John D. Negroponte, "Threats, Challenges, and Opportunities for the U.S." Annual Threat Assessment to the Senate Select Committee on Intelligence, Washington, D.C., February 2, 2006.

Negroponte is the director of National Intelligence.

66Al Qaeda's ubiquity and capacity to do damage may have, as with so many perceived threats, been exaggerated. Just because some terrorists may wish to do great harm does not mean that they are able to.99

—John Mueller, "Is There Still a Terrorist Threat? The Myth of the Omnipresent Enemy," *Foreign Affairs,* September/ October 2006.

Mueller is a professor of political science at Ohio State University and the author of *The Remnants of War.*

66 Given North Korea's economic strains, it is conceivable that it could be motivated to sell nuclear materials to other states or even terrorist groups if the price is right. 99

—Joseph Cirincione and Jon B. Wolfsthal, "North Korea and Iran: Test Cases for an Improved Nonproliferation Regime?" *Arms Control Today*, December 2003.

Cirincione is director and Wolfsthal is deputy director of the Non-Proliferation Project at the Carnegie Endowment for International Peace. They are authors of *Deadly Arsenals: Tracking Weapons of Mass Destruction.*

66 It is significant that Iran has possessed chemical weapons for decades, yet there is no indication that it has passed on any of those weapons to Hezbollah or to Palestinian groups that Tehran supports politically. Why should one assume that the mullahs would be more reckless with nuclear weapons? 99

—Ted Galen Carpenter, "Iran's Nuclear Program: America's Policy Options," Cato Institute, *Policy Analysis,* no. 578, September 20, 2006.

Carpenter is vice president for defense and foreign policy studies at the Cato Institute and the author of *Peace and Freedom: Foreign Policy for a Constitutional Republic.*

Facts and Illustrations

Is the United States Likely to Be Attacked with Nuclear Weapons?

- Approximately **525 nuclear explosions** have occurred aboveground since Hiroshima, but not one has been an act of war.

- According to former U. S. ambassador to NATO Robert E. Hunter, aside from the Soviet transfer of some uranium to China in the 1950s, no country with bomb-making **fissionable materials** has knowingly transferred them to anyone else.

- According to a 2006 *Foreign Policy* poll of more than **100 experts** and officials:
    - **47 percent** view loose nuclear materials and weapons as the greatest threat to U.S. national security;
    - **32 percent** view al Qaeda and terrorism as the greatest threat to U.S. national security;
    - just **4 percent** view Iran as the greatest threat;
    - more than two-thirds (**66 percent**) believed stopping the proliferation of nuclear weapons to rogue states should be a higher priority in fighting the war on terror.

- According to an AP-Ipsos poll taken in September 2005, **53 percent** of Americans think a nuclear attack by terrorists is somewhat likely to occur within the United States.

- World stockpiles of nuclear weapons have declined by more than **66 percent** since the 1960s.

Is the United States Likely to Be Attacked by Nuclear Weapons?

- For more than a decade North Koreans have suffered from famine and acute food shortages. **Hundreds of thousands** have died of starvation, and millions have suffered from chronic malnutrition.

- In 2003 President George W. Bush named North Korea, Iran, and Iraq as part of an **"Axis of Evil"** due to their determination to obtain nuclear weapons and their potential inclination to distribute them to terrorists.

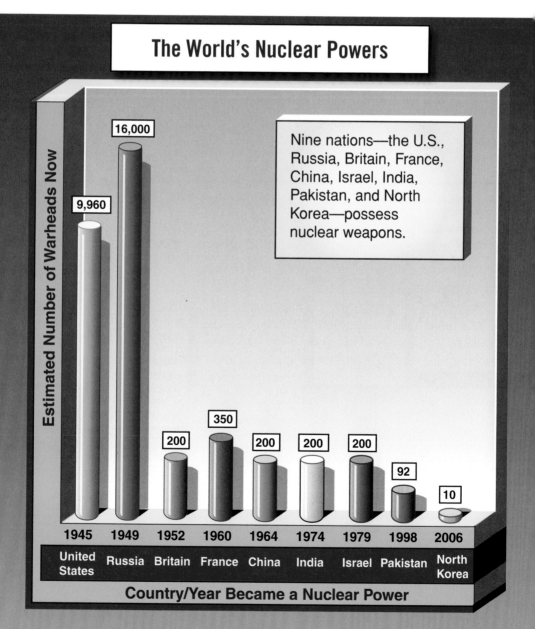

The World's Nuclear Powers

Nine nations—the U.S., Russia, Britain, France, China, Israel, India, Pakistan, and North Korea—possess nuclear weapons.

Estimated Number of Warheads Now

| 9,960 | 16,000 | 200 | 350 | 200 | 200 | 200 | 92 | 10 |

| 1945 | 1949 | 1952 | 1960 | 1964 | 1974 | 1979 | 1998 | 2006 |
| United States | Russia | Britain | France | China | India | Israel | Pakistan | North Korea |

Country/Year Became a Nuclear Power

Source: Global Nuclear Stockpiles, 1945–2006, *Bulletin of the Atomic Scientists*, July/Aug, 2006.

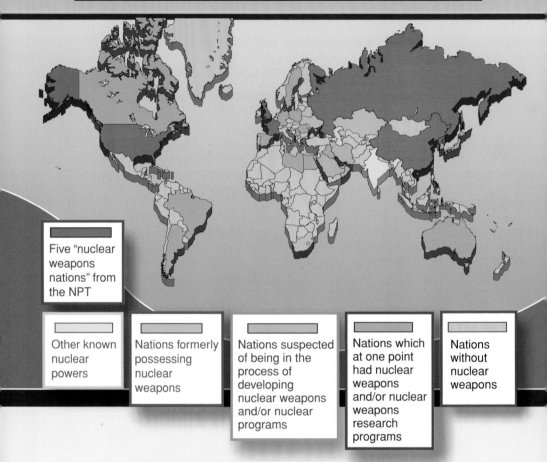

Global Status of Nuclear Weapons

Though there are just nine nuclear nations (and just five allowed by international law), a multitude of nations are at different stages of developing nuclear weapons, while others have abandoned their nuclear weapons programs.

Five "nuclear weapons nations" from the NPT

Other known nuclear powers

Nations formerly possessing nuclear weapons

Nations suspected of being in the process of developing nuclear weapons and/or nuclear programs

Nations which at one point had nuclear weapons and/or nuclear weapons research programs

Nations without nuclear weapons

Source: Nuclear Weapon Archive, 2007. http://nuclearweaponarchive.org.

- The total global nuclear weapons stockpile has been reduced from the 1986 Cold War high of more than **70,000 warheads** to about 27,000 warheads, its lowest level in 45 years.

- Of these warheads, **12,500** are considered operational, with the rest in reserve or retired and awaiting dismantlement.

Is the United States Likely to Be Attacked by Nuclear Weapons?

- Since the 1960s the number of **nuclear weapons states** has grown from five to nine—the United States, France, China, Great Britain, Russia, India, Pakistan, North Korea, and unofficially Israel.

- Of all the world's nuclear weapons, **95 percent** are in U.S. and Russian stockpiles.

Unsecured Nuclear Materials Pose the Greatest Threat to the United States

A 2006 *Foreign Policy* poll of more than 100 foreign policy experts and officials found that the majority believe unsecured nuclear material and weapons pose the greatest threat to U.S. national security.

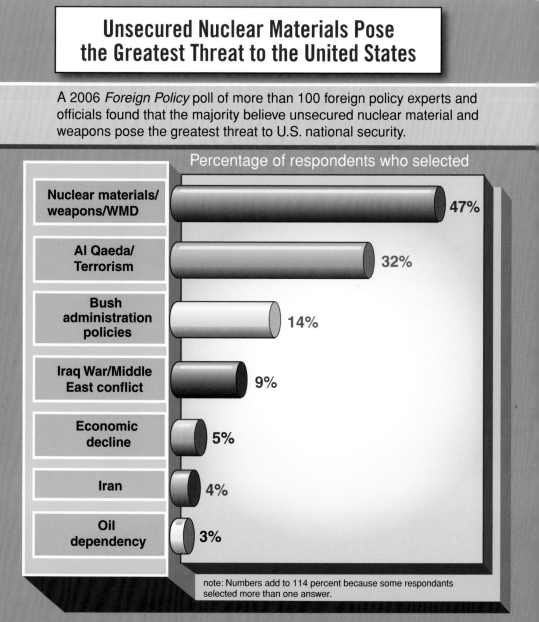

Percentage of respondents who selected

Nuclear materials/weapons/WMD	47%
Al Qaeda/Terrorism	32%
Bush administration policies	14%
Iraq War/Middle East conflict	9%
Economic decline	5%
Iran	4%
Oil dependency	3%

note: Numbers add to 114 percent because some respondants selected more than one answer.

Source: *Foreign Policy* and the Center for American Progress, "The Terrorism Index," July/August 2006.

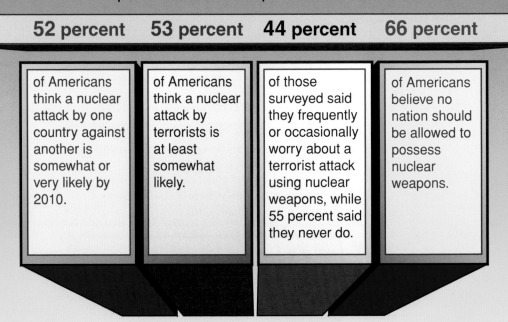

American Opinions on Nuclear Weapons

According to a 2005 Associated Press-Ipsos poll on nuclear weapons and terrorism:

52 percent	53 percent	44 percent	66 percent
of Americans think a nuclear attack by one country against another is somewhat or very likely by 2010.	of Americans think a nuclear attack by terrorists is at least somewhat likely.	of those surveyed said they frequently or occasionally worry about a terrorist attack using nuclear weapons, while 55 percent said they never do.	of Americans believe no nation should be allowed to possess nuclear weapons.

Source: Will Lester, "Most Americans Say No Nations Should Have Nuclear Weapons," Associated Press, March 31, 2005.

- Though Israel has not acknowledged it possesses nuclear weapons, the **Defense Intelligence Agency** (DIA) estimates it has between 60 and 85 warheads.

- Russia is estimated to have about **5,830** operational nuclear weapons.

- Britain is estimated to have about **200** operational nuclear weapons.

- The French nuclear stockpile includes approximately **350** warheads.

- North Korea is estimated to have between **6 and 10** nuclear weapons.

- China is estimated to have a nuclear arsenal of about **200** nuclear warheads.

How Can the Spread of Nuclear Weapons Be Prevented?

> 66 Preventing the spread of nuclear weapons is the most important challenge facing our world. No responsible person can dissent from that statement as the consequences of failure are beyond measure and constitute not merely a threat to our national survival but to civilization itself. 99

—Henry J. Hyde, Republican representative from Illinois.

> 66 It is important to recognize that the spread of nuclear weapons is a condition over which we do not have control and for which there is no solution. . . . The world is an unsafe place, and we have no choice but to live in it. 99

—William Langewiesche, *Los Angeles Times.*

The first step to preventing a nuclear catastrophe is to tightly control access to nuclear weapons and fissile materials. Since the end of the Cold War, several tactics have been used to prevent nuclear weapons from falling into the wrong hands and to prevent new nations from becoming nuclear.

Disarming the Superpowers

One of the main methods used to reduce the spread of nuclear weapons is to reduce the number of weapons that exist. Since the United States and Russia own 95 percent of all existing nuclear weapons, a series of treaties have been negotiated aimed at reducing, dismantling, or destroying their nuclear weapon and missile stocks. One of the most critical of these is the Nuclear Non-Proliferation Treaty, which went into effect in 1970. The NPT prohibits nuclear nations from helping others attain nuclear weapons and prohibits nonnuclear-weapons states from developing nuclear weapons. Nearly 190 nations had signed the treaty as of 2007. Another, more recent nonproliferation treaty was the 2002 Moscow Treaty in which the former Cold War foes agreed to reduce their respective holdings of strategic nuclear warheads to a level of 1,700–2,200 each by December 2012 (together they currently have about 10,000).

However, efforts to disarm leftover nuclear weapons from the Cold War era lapsed with the presidency of George W. Bush and the September 11 attacks on America. Arguing that the treaties were signed in a political era no longer relevant to threats faced by the United States, Bush took steps to weaken the agreements, saying such treaties "hinder our government's ability to develop ways to protect our people from future terrorist or rogue state missile attacks."[35] Indeed, since 2002 the United States has withdrawn from or let expire several important nuclear weapons treaties that have kept the arms race in check for decades. In 2002, for example, the United States withdrew from the Anti-Ballistic Missile Treaty it signed with Russia in 1972, which had forbidden the testing and deployment of ballistic missile defense systems. The United States also indicated its willingness to let the 1991 U.S.-Russia Strategic Arms Reduction Treaty (START) expire. This treaty places restrictions on nuclear warhead delivery systems and expires in 2009.

> Since 2002 the United States has withdrawn from or let expire several important nuclear weapons treaties that have kept the arms race in check for decades.

Bush and his supporters argue that the United States cannot have its hands tied as it tries to defend against terrorist enemies, who would never abide by any treaty that would weaken their arsenals. Others, however, worry that dissolving the restraints on nuclear weapons would dangerously raise the risk of nuclear war and encourage the increase of nuclear weapons around the globe. As two nuclear proliferation experts warned of the demise of the treaties, "We are a few years from the complete deregulation of the system of nuclear constraints."[36]

Protecting the Arsenal of the Former Soviet Union

Another key tactic in preventing the spread of nuclear weapons is to safeguard the former Soviet Union's nuclear arsenal. In the chaotic collapse of the Soviet Union, many of its nuclear weapons storage facilities were left unguarded, and the status of many weapons is unknown. In the years since the collapse in 1991, several initiatives have aimed at accounting for, securing, and dismantling the former superpower's nuclear arsenal. The most important of these efforts is known as the Nunn-Lugar Cooperative Threat Reduction Program.

Funded by the United States, the Nunn-Lugar program helps the Russians pay for deactivation of nuclear warheads, for tightened security surrounding nuclear facilities, and for employment of nuclear scientists who might otherwise sell their services to terrorists. It is believed the program significantly reduces the chance of loose weapons being stolen or sold

> " The Nunn-Lugar program helps the Russians pay for deactivation of nuclear warheads, for tightened security surrounding nuclear facilities, and for employment of nuclear scientists who might otherwise sell their services to terrorists. "

to terrorists and prevents talented scientists' collaborating with terrorists out of financial need. Said Senator Richard G. Lugar, one of the founding fathers of the program:

> We must perfect a worldwide system of accountability for nuclear, biological, and chemical weapons. In such a system, every nation that currently has weapons and materials of mass destruction must account for what it has, safely secure what it has, and demonstrate that no other nation or cell will be allowed access.

> Meanwhile, we must work to contract existing stockpiles and prevent further proliferation. If a nation lacks the means to participate in this effort, the international community must provide financial and technical assistance.[37]

As of 2005, programs funded by the Nunn-Lugar program had deactivated or destroyed 6,760 nuclear warheads, 789 nuclear air-to-surface missiles, 28 nuclear submarines, 194 nuclear test tunnels, and thousands of other nuclear-weapons-related items.

Also, funding from Nunn-Lugar has helped former nuclear weapons scientists and engineers find employment on peaceful projects. According to the 2005 Nunn-Lugar report, 58,000 former weapons scientists have been employed in peaceful work. A related program, the International Proliferation Prevention Program, has funded 750 projects that employ 14,000 former weapons scientists and has created 580 new non-weapons-related jobs. Some of these jobs relate to nuclear power for peaceful purposes, while others will work on cutting-edge medical technologies. Of these programs Linton Brooks, ambassador of the U.S. National Nuclear Security Administration, has said, "We're continuing our programs to develop commercial projects to employ ex-Soviet weapons scientists. This program has reaped enormous industrial and medical benefits, and continues to grow in new and interesting ways."[38]

Disarmament and employment programs have been instituted in regions outside the former Soviet Union as well. In 2004 Bush pledged $20 billion over 10 years that will be spent protecting weapons of mass destruction and employing scientists and technicians from countries such as Iraq and Libya, both of which no longer have operating nuclear weapons programs.

Containing Rogue States That Seek Nuclear Weapons

Perhaps the most critical method for preventing nuclear weapons proliferation is keeping hostile nations from acquiring or developing them. Both North Korea and Iran have been fingered as the two states most likely to use nuclear weapons in an attack or to give, sell, or allow nuclear weapons or fissile materials in their possession to be transferred to terrorists.

To the chagrin of the international community, North Korea successfully tested a nuclear bomb on October 9, 2006, and claims it has enough fissile material to make about 6 to 10 bombs (although experts believe none of them are large enough to be launched with a missile). Iran has yet to acquire nuclear weapons, although it is believed to be working hard to acquire the technology with which to make them. Iran claims that its efforts are peaceful in nature, that it only seeks nuclear power technology to provide electricity for its 68 million citizens. But given Iran's contentious history with the West, its open support for terrorist groups such as Hizballah, its numerous declarations of hatred for Israel and the United States, and its need to defend itself in an increasingly militarized region, the United Nations, United States, and much of Europe are suspicious that Iran seeks nuclear technology for military rather than civilian purposes.

> **The Six-Party Talks are aimed at getting North Korea to abandon its nuclear program in exchange for food, aid, and medicine, which it badly needs.**

Indeed, the international community and the United States in particular has identified these two nations as presenting a particular threat to the international community. In 2001 Bush declared both states to be part of an "Axis of Evil" and has repeatedly warned he will not permit "dangerous regimes to threaten us with the world's most deadly weapons."[39]

Waging Diplomacy

The international community has pursued several strategies for containing North Korea and Iran. One used regularly with North Korea is diplomacy, specifically diplomacy pursued through talks between North Korea and China, Japan, South Korea, Russia, and the United States. These talks, known as the Six-Party Talks, began in 2003 after North Korea withdrew from the Nuclear Non-Proliferation Treaty, which prohibited it from developing nuclear weapons. Not wanting the hostile and isolated North Korean regime led by Kim Jong Il to be in possession of such weapons, the talks are aimed at getting North Korea to abandon its nuclear program in exchange for food, aid, and medicine, which it badly needs.

> It is argued that because North Korea in reality only has enough weapons to threaten its neighbors, the United States should take the lead in disarming the contentious state.

The Six-Party Talks has had a few successes over the years, such as in 2005 when North Korea agreed to shut down all of its existing nuclear programs for a hefty aid package. But a breakdown in diplomacy and efforts by the United States to resist being essentially blackmailed resulted in North Korea's successful acquisition of nuclear weapons in 2006. After this development many wondered what could be done to prevent North Korea from using or selling its new technology. Some believed, again, that diplomacy was the best method. As Robert L. Galluci put it, "It may be righteous, denying North Korea the reward of bilateral talks, but it has failed to secure U.S. interests."[40]

Some, such as Brookings scholar Susan E. Rice, have urged the United States to engage in a full-fledged diplomatic relationship with the North Koreans, arguing that "rolling back North Korea's nuclear program is more important to U.S. national security than any principled objection to direct negotiations or tacit ambitions to change that odious regime." Rice urges the United States to

> immediately propose high-level, bilateral talks and personally confirm that the United States has 'no hostile intent' toward North Korea. In exchange for the 'complete, verifiable and irreversible' dismantling of North Korea's nuclear programs, the United States should offer security guarantees, economic ties, fuel supplies and diplomatic relations.[41]

Yet others believe it is not the job of the United States to take the lead in convincing North Korea to abandon its weapons program. The United States has long been criticized for acting as "the world's policeman," a role that makes it globally unpopular and stretches its resources, military, and budget. It is argued that because North Korea in reality only has enough weapons to threaten its neighbors, they should take the lead in disarming the contentious state. Argue foreign policy experts Anatol Lieven and

John Hulsman, "North Korea must be treated as a regional problem to be managed by a regional concert of powers, with China in the lead. The U.S. role in all this should be sympathetic—and distant."[42]

Sanctions: Nuclear Deterrent or Immoral Punitive Tool?

Sanctions are another tool the international community can use to dissuade both North Korea and Iran from developing or disseminating weapons of mass destruction. Sanctions are a set of rules imposed on a nation or group of nations that prevent them from trading or providing certain goods to a country being punished for breaking international law. Sanctions have long been used to put pressure on a rogue government and convince it to comply with international rules; the idea being that if a government is denied access to certain products, it will be willing to change its behavior.

Following North Korea's October 2006 nuclear test, the United Nations immediately took actions to impose sanctions against it. In a rare show of unity, the UN Security Council (composed of 5 permanent member states that each possess nuclear weapons—the United States, Russia, China, the United Kingdom, and France—and 10 rotating member states) voted unanimously to pass Draft Resolution 1718, which imposed a strict set of sanctions on North Korea. Under these rules no member state is allowed to supply North Korea with military supplies or any technological materials that could help it continue its weapons program. It also prevents the trade of luxury goods as a way to punish the North Korean leadership for its violation of UN rules. The UN adopted the resolution to punish North Korea's defiance, to prevent it from further developing its weapons

> " Sanctions have long been used to put pressure on a rogue government and convince it to comply with international rules; the idea being that if a government is denied access to certain products, it will be willing to change its behavior. "

> **[Some] point out that isolating a nation with sanctions usually just serves to strengthen, rather than weaken, its leader's grip on the country.**

program, to pressure it to return to international talks, and to show other nations that are considering developing nuclear weapons that there are consequences for violating international law.

The efficacy of sanctions is hotly debated. Some believe that squeezing a nation of needed products and supplies is the best way to get its government to comply with international law. A successful example of this strategy occurred in 2003, when Libyan leader Muammar al-Gaddafi agreed to abolish Libya's nuclear weapons programs after being subject to strict sanctions and international isolation. Indeed, the sanctions set against North Korea were meant to achieve the same effect. To some level they have succeeded: A month after the UN adopted the sanctions set down in Resolution 1718, North Korea agreed to return to the Six-Party Talks and to shut down its nuclear facilities in exchange for 50,000 tons of heavy fuel oil and normalized relationships with the United States and Japan. Said Bush of the sanctions, "This action by the United Nations, which was swift and tough, says that we are united in our determination to see to it that the Korean Peninsula is nuclear-weapons free."[43]

But others argue that sanctions are not a useful tool. They point out that isolating a nation with sanctions usually just serves to strengthen, rather than weaken, its leader's grip on the country. Indeed, the more a people are isolated and the less exposure they have to outside goods and services, the more reliant they become on the regime. To be sure, sanctions prevent products from entering North Korea and spurring ideas that might broaden the North Korean people's perspective, which could lead them to overthrow the regime. As author Nicholas D. Kristof explains, "Look around the world at the regimes we despise: North Korea, Cuba, Burma and Iran. Those are among the world's most long-lived regimes, and that's partly because the sanctions and isolation we have imposed on them have actually propped them up—by giving those countries' leaders an excuse for their economic failures and a chance to cloak themselves in nationalism."[44]

Furthermore, it is often argued that sanctions punish the people who deserve it least: the citizens. When goods, services, and other products are withheld from a country, it is usually the leaders of the country who feel it last. With private reserves and connections, the wealthy and powerful can fend for themselves; it is the poor masses that tend to be hit hardest by the deprivation of products. Write foreign policy experts Ted Galen Carpenter and Christopher Preble, "It is typical of economic sanctions that they hurt the most vulnerable members of society. Indeed, this fatally undermines the effectiveness of sanctions."[45]

Going to War to Prevent the Spread of Weapons

A final option for dealing with states seeking or possessing nuclear weapons is war. It has been suggested that both the North Korean and Iranian nuclear facilities be taken out with a military strike, or full-on war be declared to overthrow those regimes intent on pursuing weapons of mass destruction without the permission of the international community.

The reality of the United States going to war to disarm Iran or North Korea is unlikely. One reason is that U.S. troops are bogged down in the war in Iraq. The unpopularity of that war and its failure to have much effect on the nuclear proliferation problem has led many to view military action as a highly undesirable method of preventing the spread of nuclear weapons. One author describes the sheer impossibility of an attack on Iran to halt its nuclear program. "Were America to take preemptive action, America would also have to be willing and ready to occupy Iran to diffuse Iran's anger at having been struck. Even if it were possible to pacify a nation the size of Iran after such an attack, given its global commitments, America is in no position now to do that and thus cooler heads must prevail."[46]

But others, such as William Kristol, editor of the conservative newsmagazine the *Weekly Standard,* argue that in order for U.S. pressure on Iran to be effective

> Sanctions punish the people who deserve it least: the citizens. When goods, services, and other products are withheld from a country, it is usually the leaders of the country who feel it last.

> **War against North Korea, Iran, and other nuclear weapons proliferators remains a last resort among politicians, diplomats and military strategists.**

it must be backed up with the threat of military action. "The only way diplomatic, political, and economic pressure has a chance to work . . . is if the military option—or various military options—are kept on the table," says Kristol. Therefore, "we support holding open the possibility of, and beginning to prepare for, various forms of military action."[47]

War against North Korea, Iran, and other nuclear weapons proliferators remains a last resort among politicians, diplomats, and military strategists, however. Officials will continue to pursue the methods that have worked to curb nuclear weapons proliferation for decades—sanctions, diplomacy, and international treaties—in the hope of preventing the world's most dangerous weapons from falling into the wrong hands.

How Can the Spread of Nuclear Weapons Be Prevented?

66 The invasion of Iran is out of the question: Iran is three times the size and population of Iraq, the terrain is far more mountainous, the people are more united against foreign attack, and—unlike Iraq in 2003—no sanctions have been in place preventing the country from maintaining and strengthening its military arsenal. 99

—Stephen Zunes, "The Iranian Nuclear Threat: Myth and Reality," *Tikkun,* January/February 2007.

Zunes is a professor of political science at the University of San Francisco and the author of *Tinderbox: U.S. Middle East Policy and the Roots of Terrorism.*

66 Doves profess concern about Iran's nuclear program and endorse various diplomatic responses to it. But they don't want even to contemplate the threat of military action. Perhaps military action won't ultimately be necessary. But the only way diplomatic, political, and economic pressure has a chance to work over the next months is if the military option—or various military options—are kept on the table. 99

—William Kristol, "And Now Iran; We Can't Rule Out the Use of Military Force," *Weekly Standard,* January 23, 2006.

Kristol is the editor of the *Weekly Standard,* a conservative political magazine.

Bracketed quotes indicate conflicting positions.

* Editor's Note: While the definition of a primary source can be narrowly or broadly defined, for the purposes of Compact Research, a primary source consists of: 1) results of original research presented by an organization or researcher; 2) eyewitness accounts of events, personal experience, or work experience; 3) first-person editorials offering pundits' opinions; 4) government officials presenting political plans and/or policies; 5) representatives of organizations presenting testimony or policy.

Primary Source Quotes

❝I'm not recommending it but, on the other hand, it is a grave step to tolerate a world of multiple nuclear-weapons centers without restraint. I'm not recommending military action, but I'm recommending not excluding it.❞

—Henry Kissinger, interviewed by Bernard Gwertzman, "Kissinger: Don't Exclude Military Action Against Iran If Negotiations Fail," Council on Foreign Relations, July 14, 2005. www.cfr.org.

Kissinger is an American diplomat and politician famous for his hard-line foreign policies during the Vietnam War and the Cold War.

❝At most, [military] strikes would delay, not eliminate, Tehran's program. There is also a grave risk that Iran would retaliate . . . including attacks against U.S. forces in Iraq and through proxy organizations. Attacking Iran would also further alienate Muslim populations around the world, creating the very real prospect of a war of civilizations.❞

—Ted Galen Carpenter, "Iran's Nuclear Program: America's Policy Options," Cato Institute, *Policy Analysis,* no. 578, September 20, 2006.

Carpenter is the vice president for defense and foreign policy studies at the Cato Institute and the coauthor of *The Korean Conundrum: America's Troubled Relations with North and South Korea.*

❝All of today's great powers share an interest in the proposed campaign [to prevent the spread of nuclear weapons]. Each has sufficient reasons to fear nuclear weapons in terrorists' hands, whether they are al Qaeda, Chechens, or Chinese separatists.❞

—Graham Allison, "How to Stop Nuclear Terror," *Foreign Affairs,* January/February 2004.

Allison is a former assistant secretary of defense for policy and plans under President Bill Clinton and currently teaches at Harvard's Kennedy School of Government.

66We know that the terrorists, and some of those who support them, seek the ability to deliver death and destruction to our doorstep via missile. And we must have the freedom and the flexibility to develop effective defenses against those attacks. Defending the American people is my highest priority as Commander in Chief, and I cannot and will not allow the United States to remain in a treaty that prevents us from developing effective defenses.99

—George W. Bush, "Remarks by the President on National Missile Defense, December 13, 2001. www.whitehouse.gov.

Bush is the 43rd President of the United States. He gave these remarks when he announced America's intention to withdraw from the 1972 Antiballistic Missile Treaty.

66At a time when both states and terrorist groups have clear nuclear ambitions, America has no choice but to lead responsibly toward radically reducing the role of nuclear weapons. . . . It is time to substantially reduce weapons stockpiles, ratify a test-ban treaty, and galvanize the international community towards coordinated action to ensure that the 60-year-old taboo against nuclear use is never broken.99

—Dennis M. Gormley, "Securing Nuclear Obsolescence," *Survival*, Autumn 2006.

Gormley is a political affairs professor at the University of Pittsburgh and a senior fellow at the Monterey Institute's Center for Nonproliferation Studies.

66In the long run, North Korea's nuclear weapons are an overwhelming problem only for its neighbors, and it should be their responsibility to sort this problem out.99

—Anatol Lieven and John Hulsman, "North Korea Isn't Our Problem," *Los Angeles Times*, October 11, 2006.

Lieven is a senior research fellow at the New America Foundation in Washington, D.C. Hulsman is a scholar in residence at the German Council on Foreign Relations in Berlin. Their new book is titled *Ethical Realism: A Vision for America's Role in the World.*

“Despite all the disagreement over who's to blame for the North Korean nuclear test, everyone agrees on the next step: economic sanctions. But does anyone really think that they will work? North Korea is already the most isolated country in the world. Its people live at subsistence levels, escaping mass starvation only because of aid shipments. There is virtually no industrial economy.... [Sanctions] have not stopped the regime from acquiring nuclear weapons. Nor have they loosened the regime's grip on power.”

—Fareed Zakaria, "Let Them Eat Carrots: America Has Used Sanctions Since the 1950s, but Nothing Has Stopped North Korea from Getting the Bomb," *Newsweek,* October 23, 2006.

Zakaria is a columnist for *Newsweek* and the editor of *Newsweek International.*

“The biggest threat to North Korea's regime isn't from American warships, but from the sight of other Koreans dieting, or listening on iPods to love songs, or watching decadent television comedies. So let's stop helping the Dear Leader isolate his own people.”

—Nicholas D. Kristof, "Send in the Fat Guys," *New York Times,* October 22, 2006.

Kristof is a columnist for the *New York Times.*

“A 'Global Cleanout Campaign' should [be undertaken to] extract all nascent nukes from all other countries within the next 12 months. Since all research reactors in non-nuclear weapons states contain fissile material that came from either the United States or Russia, each has a sufficient legal claim to demand its return.”

—Graham Allison, "How to Stop Nuclear Terror," *Foreign Affairs,* January/February 2004.

Allison is a former assistant secretary of defense for policy and plans under President Bill Clinton and currently teaches at Harvard's Kennedy School of Government.

How Can the Spread of Nuclear Weapons Be Prevented?

- As of 2005, programs funded by the **Nunn-Lugar program** have deactivated or destroyed:
  - **6,760** nuclear warheads
  - **587** Intercontinental ballistic missiles (ICBMs)
  - **483** ICBM storage silos
  - **32** ICBM mobile missile launchers
  - **150** bombers
  - **789** nuclear air-to-surface missiles
  - **436** submarine missile launchers
  - **549** submarine-launched missiles
  - **28** nuclear submarines
  - **194** nuclear test tunnels

- As a result of Nunn-Lugar, Ukraine, Belarus, and Kazakhstan are **nuclear-weapons** free. They otherwise would be the world's third, fourth, and eighth largest nuclear weapons powers, respectively.

- The International Proliferation Prevention Program has funded **750** projects and **580** jobs involving **14,000** former nuclear weapons scientists.

- Compared with its forces in 1990, in 2006 Moscow had **55 percent** fewer intercontinental ballistic missiles, **39 percent** fewer strategic bombers, and **80 percent** fewer ballistic-missile submarines.

Nuclear Weapons Development in Iran

In 2005, Iran resumed its nuclear weapons program over the objections of the international community. Although weapons inspectors have not been allowed into the country, it is suspected that several Iranian cities contain facilities dedicated to nuclear weapons research and development.

Source: "An Overview of Nuclear Weapons Facilities in Iran, Israel, and Turkey," Greenpeace, February 2007.

North Korea's Nuclear Weapons Facilities

Reportedly North Korea has as many as 22 nuclear facilities in 18 locations. These include uranium mines, refinery plants, nuclear fuel plants, nuclear reactors, reprocessing facilities, and research facilities.

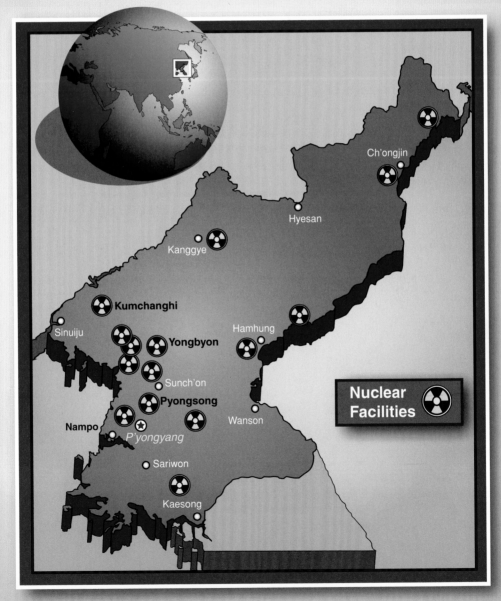

Source: www.globalsecurity.org, April 2007.

- Russia has about **8,800** warheads awaiting dismantlement.

- According to a June 2006 *Los Angeles Times*/Bloomberg poll, **56 percent** of Americans believe Iran will acquire nuclear weapons despite sanctions or diplomatic efforts.

Spending Millions to Safeguard Old Soviet Nuclear Resources

The Nunn-Lugar Cooperative Threat Reduction Program has spent billions of dollars since 1992 working to secure old Soviet nuclear stockpiles and employ former scientists and engineers.

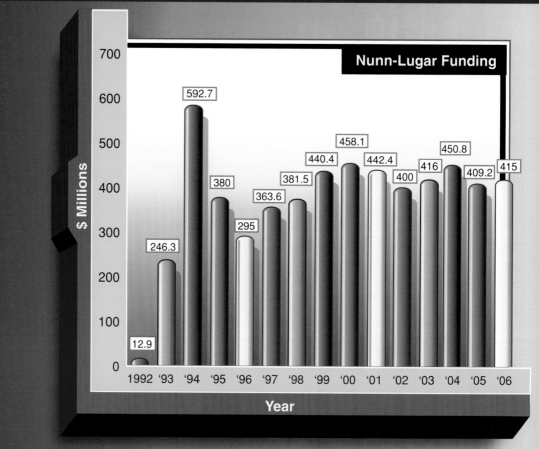

Source: Nunn-Lugar Report, August 2005. http://lugar.senate.gov.

Thousands of Nuclear Materials Have Been Safeguarded

The Nunn-Lugar Cooperative Threat Reduction (CTR) Program has safeguarded the following nuclear materials from Soviet stockpiles. It projects even more success from 2007 through 2012.

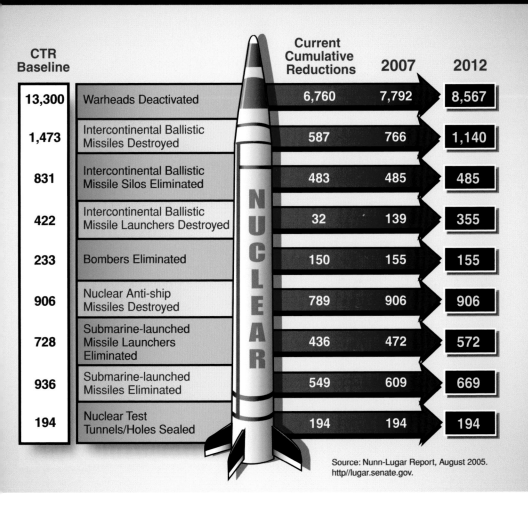

CTR Baseline		Current Cumulative Reductions	2007	2012
13,300	Warheads Deactivated	6,760	7,792	8,567
1,473	Intercontinental Ballistic Missiles Destroyed	587	766	1,140
831	Intercontinental Ballistic Missile Silos Eliminated	483	485	485
422	Intercontinental Ballistic Missile Launchers Destroyed	32	139	355
233	Bombers Eliminated	150	155	155
906	Nuclear Anti-ship Missiles Destroyed	789	906	906
728	Submarine-launched Missile Launchers Eliminated	436	472	572
936	Submarine-launched Missiles Eliminated	549	609	669
194	Nuclear Test Tunnels/Holes Sealed	194	194	194

Source: Nunn-Lugar Report, August 2005.
http//lugar.senate.gov.

- According to a June 2006 *CBS News* poll, **22 percent** of Americans believe military action is the best way to confront the nuclear threat from Iran.

- According to a May 2006 *Fox News*/Opinion Dynamics poll, **74 percent** believe the United Nations cannot stop Iran from acquiring the technology to build nuclear weapons.

- On **October 9, 2006**, the North Korean government successfully conducted a nuclear test, showing the world it possessed nuclear weapons.

- Both the United States Geologic Survey and Japanese seismological authorities detected the equivalent of a **4.2 magnitude earthquake** in North Korea, indicating the detonation of a small bomb.

- North Korea is believed to have between **6 and 10 small nuclear weapons** in its arsenal.

- On **October 14, 2006**, the United Nations Security Council passed a resolution imposing sanctions on North Korea for its October 9, 2006, nuclear test. UN Resolution 1718 banned the sale of luxury goods to North Korea, which include automobiles, liquor, cigarettes, melons, beef, and home electronic goods.

- According to the Natural Resources Defense Council's Nuclear Notebook, the CIA, the Defense Intelligence Agency, and the Pentagon:
  - As of 2006 the United States had a total of **9,962** nuclear weapons stationed in locations within the United States and around the world.
  - This includes **5,735** active or operational warheads: **5,235** strategic and 500 nonstrategic warheads.
  - Approximately **4,225** additional warheads are held in the reserve or inactive stockpiles, some of which will be dismantled. Some **4,365** warheads are scheduled to be retired for dismantlement by 2012.
  - Since 1997 the **Pentagon** has removed nuclear weapons from three states (California, Virginia, and South Dakota).
  - 1n 1991 the United States withdrew all of its **nuclear weapons** from South Korea and thousands more from Europe in 1993.
  - The army and Marine Corps **denuclearized** in the early 1990s.

How Can the United States Defend Itself Against a Nuclear Attack?

❝The U.S. remains woefully unprepared for a catastrophic nuclear attack on one major American city let alone six or seven.❞

—K. Chandler, reporter for the Florida daily paper *Westside Gazette.*

❝It may be possible to develop a multi-element, layered, global, civil/military system of systems and capabilities that would greatly reduce the likelihood of a successful clandestine nuclear attack.❞

—Defense Science Board Task Force, conclusions of declassified 2004 report *Preventing and Defending Against Clandestine Nuclear Attack.*

Any nuclear attack, even a small scale one, would likely cause mass destruction and death. Therefore, first responders and military strategists believe that the best way to defend against a nuclear attack is to prevent one from occurring. But in lieu of preventing terrorists or rogue nations from acquiring nuclear weapons, the United States has several ways to thwart or deal with a nuclear attack should one be attempted.

Detecting Radiation at the Nation's Borders

One way to prevent a nuclear attack in America's homeland is to prevent a weapon from being brought into the country. Although some experts debate whether terrorists could realistically obtain a nuclear weapon or materials to build one, many believe it is prudent to guard the borders in the event it happens. After all, many nuclear weapons are small and lightweight, weighing only around 300 pounds. A weapon that size could be easily transported in a car, van, truck, or ship. Amounts of radioactive material that could be used to make a dirty bomb might also be smuggled in this way, so authorities have spent millions setting up radioactive monitors at various checkpoints along U.S. points of entry.

The United States has made great progress installing these radioactive detection facilities. Since 2003 it has spent more than $280 million dollars installing detection portals at the nation's ports, airports, and borders. It has also invested in hand-held radiation detectors that are used to swab people and cargo. As of 2006 nearly 60 percent of all "containerized" commercial goods entering the United States by truck or ship underwent screening for radioactive material; even more impressive, 77 percent of all private cars were screened. These successes led technology author Roger Allan to boast, "Today's detection and neutralization systems help guard our borders against people, cargo, and vehicles that may be carrying explosives, arms, and contraband that could include pathogenic and even nuclear material."[48]

> **Many nuclear weapons are small and lightweight, weighing only around 300 pounds. A weapon that size could be easily transported in a car, van, truck, or ship.**

Although these are big improvements over pre–September 11 levels, installation of radiation screening devices was, as of 2007, running behind schedule due to funding problems and worries about the economic effect lengthy detection processes might have on the movement of products and goods. According to reporter Eric Lipton, "So far, [only] about 670 of the planned 3,034 primary radiation detection monitors are in place, and at the rate they are being installed—22 a month on average last year [2005]—the Homeland Security Department will not meet its September 2009 goal."[49] Furthermore, the nation's railroads and freight trains were still not subject to any radiation detection monitoring.

Failing an Important Test

In an alarming example of how vulnerable the nation remains to an attack from a border-smuggled nuclear weapon, in December 2006 undercover congressional investigators successfully brought radioactive material into the country. The investigators drove across both the Canadian and Mexican borders at several locations where radiation detection equipment had been installed. The radioactive material sounded alarms, which caused the undercover agents to be pulled over for questioning. Yet border officers who interrogated them failed to find anything suspicious or to recognize the fake documents they carried supposedly authorizing the agents to carry the radioactive material. (The agents had made the fake documents using images and text pulled from Nuclear Regulatory Commission documents found on the Internet.)

> " In December 2006 undercover congressional investigators successfully brought radioactive material into the country. "

These and other failures, delays, and inconsistencies have led some to believe that pouring money, time, and attention into radiation detection border processes is not an effective use of precious homeland security resources. For one, it is debated how dangerous radioactive materials that could be smuggled by hand would even be; according to Vayl Oxford, chief of the Homeland Security Department's Domestic Nuclear Detection Office, the material smuggled in by the undercover agents would have had limited effect if used in a weapon, anyway. Secondly, radiation monitors do not always distinguish radioactivity in bomb-making substances from naturally occurring radiation, which is sometimes found in cat litter, ceramics, fertilizers, bananas, and patients who have undergone certain medical procedures. These realities have led some to believe that border radiation detection systems are simply not the best approach to preventing a nuclear attack. Says James Jay Carafano, senior fellow for national and homeland security at the Heritage Foundation: "Scanning containers full of sneakers for a 'nuke in a box' is not a really thoughtful thing."[50]

Intercepting a Nuclear Weapon on Course for the United States

In addition to sealing the nation's borders, another strategy for thwarting a nuclear attack involves shooting down a nuclear weapon on course for the United States. Indeed, since the Cold War, U.S. military strategists, politicians, and scientists have pursued technology to intercept a missile-launched nuclear weapon with another missile. Such ideas are called National Missile Defense (NMD) initiatives, and over the decades many technology systems have been installed for this purpose.

The best defense against an incoming missile-launched nuclear weapon has traditionally been the antiballistic missile (ABM). The weapon is called "antiballistic" because its job is to intercept and destroy the ballistic or intercontinental ballistic missile that would be used to deliver a nuclear weapon (and other more conventional weapons) to a target. The current NMD system consists primarily of ground-based antiballistic missiles and radar that is stationed in Alaska. About 10 of these interceptor missiles were operational as of 2006, and, because the only deployment center is located in Alaska, these ABMs would only be able to successfully intercept a nuclear weapon coming from the direction of Russia or China.

Due to the limitations of this system, the Bush administration has pursued broader defense programs that would include sea-based, high-altitude, and even space-based missile defense systems. The most ambitious and controversial of these ideas is to create an antiballistic weapons and laser system based on a satellite that would orbit in space. The idea is that if the United States detected a threat, the satellite could respond faster and more accurately than any land-based interception system. But in addition to the high cost and difficulty of perfecting the system, it has been publicly criticized. As Theresa Hitchens of the Center for Defense Information put it, "No other nation on earth is going to accept the US developing something they see as the death star. It's not going to happen. People are going to find ways to target it, and it's going to create a huge problem."[51]

While debating the creation of a space-based missile defense system, the United States has tried to broaden its missile defense abilities by collaborating with other nations. For example, in 2002 the United States requested the use of facilities in England and Denmark in an antiballistic missile defense plan and since 2002 has been in talks with Poland and other European countries to set up a European base that could intercept missiles launched from the Middle East or North Africa. Furthermore, the United States and Japan have reportedly discussed building a $3 billion missile defense shield that would comprise a network of satellites, radar, and missiles based in Japan that would be capable of locking onto missiles launched from North Korea and destroying them in mid-air.

But in general, missile defense has proven to be an enormously expensive and problematic approach to protecting the United States from a nuclear weapons attack. Missiles cost a lot of money, can fail or misfire, and, most of all, threaten to fan an arms race that heightens tensions all around the globe. Although NMD has been pursued for decades, it has yet to provide the United States with the effective security blanket it seeks.

Responding to a Nuclear Emergency

In the event a nuclear attack is not prevented at the border or by using antiballistic missiles, all states have contingency plans for this emergency. Part of the plan is to evacuate people in an affected area to shelters, although in reality, this is difficult to prepare for since the evacuation sites may themselves be affected by the blast. However, authorities could likely use early warning, satellite, and other defense technologies to glean information on where an attack will occur and how large a blast site they can expect so they can begin evacuating and sheltering people before the bomb strikes.

In addition to evacuation and providing shelter, another approach for dealing with fallout from a nuclear attack, especially one involving a nuclear power plant, is to dole out potassium iodide (KI) pills to those who may have been exposed to serious levels of radiation. According to the U.S. Nuclear Regulatory Commission, "Potassium iodide, if taken within the appropriate time and at the appropriate dosage, blocks the thyroid gland's uptake of radioactive iodine and thus reduces the risk of thyroid cancers and other diseases that might otherwise be caused by thyroid uptake of

> " The United States and Japan have reportedly discussed building a $3 billion missile defense shield which would comprise a network of satellites, radar, and missiles based in Japan that would be capable of . . .[destroying] missiles launched from North Korea. "

radioactive iodine that could be dispersed in a severe reactor accident."[52] As of 2007, 21 states had programs to dole out KI tablets to populations that reside within 10 miles of a nuclear power plant. KI tablets from the Nuclear Regulatory Commission were given to 20 states, while one, Illinois, has its own KI program in place. There remained 13 states that have populations living near nuclear power plants that do not have KI programs, although the tablets are available for public purchase.

Although KI programs are a good step toward protecting the public, they are not a panacea for exposure to radioactivity because radioactive iodine is just one of several radioactive materials that could be present in the event of a nuclear blast. Furthermore, the 10-mile zone adopted by state KI programs may not sufficiently cover all those in danger of exposure. According to some estimates, those living within as many as 300 miles of a radioactive event may be exposed to harmful levels of radiation. After the 1986 Chernobyl disaster in which a nuclear reactor leaked radiation, for example, areas of significant radiation contamination were found 20, 120, and even 300 miles from the reactor. Finally, although the drug has been approved by the Food and Drug Administration (FDA), side effects of taking KI include gastrointestinal disorders, allergic reactions, and hypothyroidism disorders, and KI may also cause damage in pregnant women and children. For these reasons health officials stress that potassium iodide pills should be taken only as a last resort and even then may not help protect Americans from the devastating effects of nuclear radiation.

Funding for many of these initiatives is supplied through Project BioShield, a law signed by President Bush in 2004 that increases funding for medical breakthroughs that protect Americans against a chemical, biological, radiological, or nuclear attack. Project BioShield has provided funding for research and development of liquid KI pills that would be safer for children and pills that would remove a greater variety of radioactive particles from the body. In September 2006 the National Institute of Allergy and Infectious Diseases (NIAID) awarded $4 million to scientists in different parts of the country pursuing these projects. "These new grants will help identify new drug candidates that could be acquired by the strategic national stockpile of medical countermeasures, which is available to the public after a terrorist or nuclear attack or accidental radioactive exposure," says NIAID director Anthony S. Fauci.[53]

Improving Public Health Systems

Getting people medical help in the event of a nuclear attack is another first line of defense against a nuclear attack, although one that would be immensely challenging. First, hospitals and trauma centers are currently unable to accommodate the volume of victims expected to be produced by a large-scale nuclear attack. As an example of just how inadequate current services would be, consider that severe burns would be a major trauma seen in the aftermath of a nuclear attack. First-degree, second-degree, and third-degree burns will occur in a multimile radius of any blast, and, depending on the population of the area hit, hundreds of thousands, even millions of people may need treatment. Yet the entire United States has facilities to treat fewer than 2,000 severe burn cases. "The hospital system has about 1,500 burn beds in the whole country, and of these maybe 80 or 90 percent are full at any given time," says scientist William Bell, co-author of a 2007 Center for Mass Destruction Defense (CMADD) report detailing the paralyzing effect a nuclear attack would have on American cities. "There's no way of treating the burn victims from a nuclear attack with the existing medical system."[54]

> The entire United States has facilities to treat fewer than 2,000 severe burn cases.

Second, most such sites exist in areas that are likely to be impacted by the nuclear blast itself. In the event of an attack they would probably be either completely destroyed or significantly disabled. For example, the CMADD study simulated a nuclear attack on the nation's capital and found that hospital systems in Washington, D.C., and the neighboring city of Baltimore, Maryland, would suffer extreme damage. A 550-kiloton bomb would cause "a 48 percent loss of hospitals in the 20 mile buffer around the two cities, a 57 percent loss of beds, and 67,000 health care workers directly affected for a total loss of 62 percent of the workers." Even a smaller, 20-kiloton bomb would cripple medical facilities: "Half of the hospitals in the immediate vicinity of the city will be circumscribed by the fallout plume."[55]

Clearly, the United States has much work to do before it is prepared to adequately respond to a nuclear attack. As the authors of the CMADD study concluded, "While we can continue to hope that large-scale mass casualties from WMD attacks will remain high consequence, low probability scenarios, it is mandatory that we invest the appropriate physical and human resources to deal with such a staggering prospect."[56] However, given the enormous devastation of even a small nuclear attack, it is fair to question whether any nation would ever be able to secure enough resources and facilities to adequately respond to the disaster. Yet politicians, scientists, medical professionals, and others will continue to make upgrades to the nation's response systems, all the while attempting to prevent a nuclear attack from ever occurring in the first place.

Primary Source Quotes*

How Can the United States Defend Itself Against a Nuclear Attack?

66 There actually is quite a bit that we can do. In certain areas, it may be possible to turn the death rate from 90 percent in some burn populations to probably 20 or 30 percent—and those are very big differences—simply by being prepared well in advance. 99

—Cham E. Dallas, in Jennifer Harper, "Study Finds U.S. Not Ready for Nuke Hit," *Washington Times,* March 21, 2007.

Dallas is director of the University of Georgia's Center for Mass Destruction Defense and coauthor of a three-year study that simulated small- and large-scale nuclear attacks on New York, Chicago, the District of Columbia, and Atlanta.

66 The U.S. remains woefully unprepared for a catastrophic nuclear attack on one major American city let alone six or seven. 99

—K. Chandler, "Al-Qaeda's Preparations for Nuclear Attack on U.S. Soil Nearing Completion, National Security Analysts Say," *Ft. Lauderdale Westside Gazette,* September 29–October 5, 2005.

Chandler is a reporter for the *Westside Gazette,* a Florida daily paper.

Bracketed quotes indicate conflicting positions.

* Editor's Note: While the definition of a primary source can be narrowly or broadly defined, for the purposes of Compact Research, a primary source consists of: 1) results of original research presented by an organization or researcher; 2) eyewitness accounts of events, personal experience, or work experience; 3) first-person editorials offering pundits' opinions; 4) government officials presenting political plans and/or policies; 5) representatives of organizations presenting testimony or policy.

Primary Source Quotes

❝One of our initiatives is our Securing the Cities Initiative, which is going to begin with New York and two other cities not yet selected, to begin to plan and deploy radiation detection equipment in the areas that are the major pathways into the cities, so that we will ultimately be able to detect a possible nuclear threat, even arising within the U.S., before that bomb or that nuclear weapon or that radiological bomb gets into a city where it could do the maximum amount of damage.❞

—Michael Chertoff, remarks at the International Association of Chiefs of Police Annual Conference, Boston, Massachusetts, October 16, 2006.

Chertoff is the secretary of homeland security.

❝The primary radiation monitors, which look like a standard tollbooth, cannot distinguish between naturally occurring radiation, sometimes found in ceramic tile or cat litter, and radioactivity in bomb-making substances.❞

—Eric Lipton, "Testers Slip Radioactive Materials over Borders ," *New York Times,* March 28, 2006. www.nytimes.com.

Eric Lipton is a reporter for the *New York Times*.

❝I don't think it's ever possible to provide a hundred-per-cent shield; I don't think ballistic-missile defense ever believed that they would be able to do that. I think that every step and every defensive layer that we put in complicates an adversary's plan to be able to [attack us with a nuclear weapon].❞

—Vayl Oxford, in Steve Coll, "The Unthinkable: Can the United States Be Made Safe from Nuclear Terrorism?" *New Yorker,* March 12, 2007.

Vayl Oxford is chief of the Homeland Security Department's Domestic Nuclear Detection Office.

> **In order to extend its deterrence concepts and defense capabilities to space, the U.S. will require development of new military capabilities for operation to, from, in and through space. . . . We know from history that every medium—air, land, and sea—has seen conflict. Reality indicates that space will be no different. Given this virtual certainty, the U.S. must develop the means both to deter and to defend against hostile acts in and from space.**

—U.S. Department of Defense, *Report of the Commission to Assess United States National Security Space Policy,* January 11, 2001. www.defenselink.mil.

The Commission to Assess United States National Security Space Policy was headed by former secretary of defense Donald Rumsfeld, who recommended the U.S. pursue a space-based antinuclear weapons program.

> **Not only will putting weapons in space be expensive, but it will also be incredibly destabilizing for the world. Already we see the tragic growth in the nuclear arms race on Earth. Will arming the heavens with weapons make us safer? Absolutely not.**

—Bruce K. Gagnon, "New Bush Policy: Weapons in Space," *Times Record,* October 24, 2006. www.space4peace.org.

Gagnon is coordinator of the Global Network Against Weapons and Nuclear Power in Space.

> **A hundred thousand doses is not nearly enough. If you really had a major attack you probably would need much more than that. One estimate we made was that we'd need 10 million doses.**

—Lee Hamilton, in Ed Bradley, "The Worst Case Scenario: Is America Ready for a Nuclear Terrorist Attack?" CBSnews. org, January 29, 2006. www.cbsnews.com.

Hamilton, vice chairman of the 9/11 Commission, reacting to the Department of Health and Human Services' decision to purchase only 100,000 doses of a cutting-edge radiation drug that could protect people in the event of a nuclear attack.

❝The effectiveness of potassium iodide as a specific blocker of thyroid radioiodine uptake is well established, as are the doses necessary for blocking uptake. As such, it is reasonable to conclude that potassium iodide will likewise be effective in reducing the risk of thyroid cancer in individuals or populations at risk for inhalation or ingestion of radioiodines.❞

—U.S. Department of Health and Human Services Food and Drug Administration Center for Drug Evaluation and Research (CDER), "Guidance Potassium Iodide as a Thyroid Blocking Agent in Radiation Emergencies," December 2001. www.fda.gov.

The Food and Drug Administration is responsible for safeguarding public health by assuring the safety of food, medicines, and other substances consumed by humans and animals.

❝Potassium iodide is a supplement to evacuation. It's not a magic pill. It's not going to cure all the ills of radiation.❞

—Jay Carey, in Jennifer Brown, "States Offer Free Pills No One Wants to Take," *Stateline.org*, June 7, 2002. www.stateline.org.

Carey is a spokesman for the Ohio Health Department.

❝The Bush administration and Congress have poured more than $5 billion into homeland security detection systems, radiological and otherwise, only to find that the best available equipment at the time was often of limited use. It has spent $300 million on an early class of radiation monitors that couldn't tell uranium from cat litter and invested $1.2 billion in airport baggage screening systems that initially were no more effective than the equipment screeners used before.❞

—Spencer S. Hsu, "U.S. Weighs How Best to Defend Against Nuclear Threats: Proven Technology vs. New Advances," *Washington Post*, April 15, 2006.

Hsu is a staff reporter for the *Washington Post*.

" The nationwide trend of locating a majority of the major urban health care institutions in downtown areas would result in a staggering loss of the total institutional health care delivery following nuclear weapon use. . . . [Furthermore], losing at least half of your health care responders in the first minute of the attack is all the more damaging because so many of the thermal and trauma injuries require immediate care and cannot wait for the time-consuming importation of replacement medical workers. "

—William C. Bell and Cham E. Dallas, "Vulnerability of Populations and the Urban Health Care Systems to Nuclear Weapon Attack—Examples from Four American Cities," *International Journal of Health Geographics,* Center for Mass Destruction Defense, University of Georgia, February 28, 2007. www.ij-healthgeographics.com.

Bell and Dallas are scientists at the Center for Mass Destruction Defense, College of Pharmacy, University of Georgia.

" Once built, nuclear weapons could be smuggled across U.S. borders with little difficulty. Of the seven million cargo containers that will arrive at U.S. ports this year, for example, only two percent will be opened for inspection. "

—Graham Allison, "How to Stop Nuclear Terror," *Foreign Affairs,* January/February 2004.

Allison is a former assistant secretary of defense for policy and plans under President Bill Clinton and currently teaches at Harvard's Kennedy School of Government.

How Can the United States Defend Itself Against a Nuclear Attack?

- The Russian A-135 **antiballistic missile system** is currently operational around Moscow. It is armed with nuclear warheads to intercept incoming missiles.

- Israel has a **national missile defense** against short- and medium-range missiles—their **Arrow missile system**.

- As of February 2005, **20 states** had received Potassium Iodide tablets from the **Nuclear Regulatory Commission** for their populations within 10 miles of a nuclear power plant. These states are: Alabama, Arizona, California, Connecticut, Delaware, Florida, Maryland, Massachusetts, Mississippi, New Hampshire, New Jersey, New York, North Carolina, Ohio, Pennsylvania, South Carolina, Tennessee, Vermont, Virginia, and West Virginia. Illinois has its own KI program in place.

- There are **103 nuclear reactors** in 34 states.

- Since 9/11 U.S. Customs and Border Protection has installed 321 **radiation detectors** in U.S. seaports.

- In order to get a reading from a **vehicle radiation detector**, a car must be driven through at **five miles per hour**.

- **Radiation detectors** can mistake the following substances for nuclear substances:
  - Banana peels
  - **Kitty litter**
  - Ceramic materials, such as tiles
  - Freshly laid pavement
  - Fertilizer

Nuclear Power Plants and Potassium Iodide Pills

There are 103 nuclear power plants in 34 states. If a nuclear power plant were to be the target of a terrorist attack, everyone living in the immediate vicinity would be susceptible to dangerous levels of radiation. Taking Potassium Iodide (KI), however, has been proven to mitigate the effects of radiation exposure. As of February 2005, 21 states had programs to distribute KI tablets to populations living within 10 miles of a nuclear power plant, although radiation could travel up to 300 miles away.

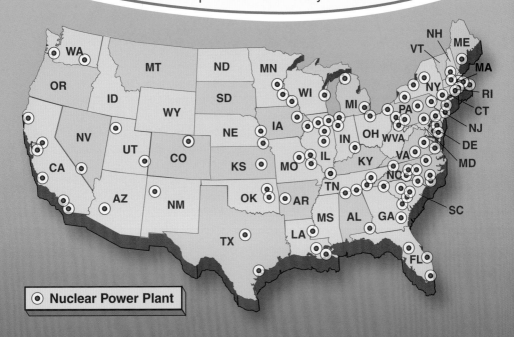

◉ **Nuclear Power Plant**

Source: *LE Magazine*, "Potassium Iodide: Insurance Against a Radiation Emergency," December 2002.

America's Largest Cities Are Likely Targets

Experts predict that terrorists are likely to target an American city that has a population of at least 100,000; there are 255 such cities in America's 50 states. The map below indicates the 25 largest cities by population.

Top 25 Targets

Population:

New York City, NY	8,213,839		
Los Angeles, CA	3,845,541	San Francisco, CA	739,426
Chicago, IL	2,842,518	Columbus, OH	730,657
Houston, TX	2,076,189	Austin, TX	690,252
Philadelphia, PA	1,463,281	Memphis, TN	672,277
Phoenix, AZ	1,461,575	Baltimore, MD	640,064
San Antonio, TX	1,256,509	Fort Worth, TX	624,067
San Diego, CA	1,255,540	Charlotte, NC	610,949
Dallas, TX	1,213,825	Nashville, TN	607,413
San Jose, CA	912,332	El Paso, TX	598,590
Detroit, MI	886,671	Boston, MA	596,638
Indianapolis, IN	784,118	Washington, D.C.	582,049
Jacksonville, FL	782,623	Milwaukee, WI	578,887

Source: *LE Magazine*, "Potassium Iodide: Insurance Against a Radiation Emergency," December 2002.

- In 2007 the Department of Homeland Security passed the **"Securing the Cities"** initiative, which mandates that radiation detectors be placed along highways, at truck stops, in weigh stations, and at other sites on the perimeter of New York City, as well as locations closer to the city center. More than **$56 million** will be spent on this effort.

- According to a **2005 Zogby poll**:
    - Two out of five Americans (**39 percent**) said preparing for a nuclear attack should be the government's top focus. This was nearly double the second-highest concern, a major disease outbreak, which was chosen by **22 percent**. Both beat natural disasters (18 percent), and environmental disasters (10 percent).
    - **48 percent** of Republicans polled believed that preparing for a nuclear attack should be the government's top responsibility.
    - **37 percent** of Democrats believed that preparing for a nuclear attack should be the government's top responsibility.
    - **33 percent** of Independents believed that preparing for a nuclear attack should be the government's top responsibility.
    - Residents of **large cities** appear to be the least concerned about preparing for nuclear attack.
    - Just **36 percent** of city residents favored devoting resources to thwarting a nuclear attack.
    - **39 percent** of small-city residents favored devoting resources to thwarting a nuclear attack.
    - **41 percent** of suburban residents favored devoting resources to thwarting a nuclear attack.
    - **42 percent** of rural area residents favored devoting resources to thwarting a nuclear attack.
    - Women are more concerned about nuclear terror than men; **45 percent** of women and 33 percent of men favor devoting resources to thwarting a nuclear terrorist attack.

Could the World Survive a Nuclear War?

"Now, I am become Death, the destroyer of worlds."

—*Bhagavad Gita,* phrase from the Hindu text quoted by physicist J. Robert Oppenheimer upon witnessing the first atomic bomb test.

"I saw something shining in the clear blue sky. I wondered what it was, so I stared at it. As the light grew bigger, the shining thing got bigger as well. And at the moment when I spoke to my friend, there was a flash, far brighter than one used for a camera. It exploded right in front of my eyes."

—Taeko Teramae, Hiroshima survivor.

Experts agree that a nuclear attack involving even just one nuclear weapon would be catastrophic. But a nuclear war—even one involving less than 0.03 percent of all nuclear weapons—would so drastically decimate natural resources and alter the planet's climate that it would spell the end of life on Earth as we know it.

What Would a Nuclear Explosion Be Like?

Some nuclear weapons are launched from great distances, using missiles that bring the warheads to their targets. Different kinds of missiles range in accuracy, speed, and size. Once the missile reaches its target, the warhead would likely be detonated about 600 to 1,500 feet above the ground in what is referred to as a "near-surface" burst.

Conversely, a nuclear weapon might be physically brought to a location and detonated on site. Indeed, many modern nuclear weapons are small and lightweight, weighing only about 300 pounds. A weapon this size could be transported to a blast site in a car or van. No matter the method of delivery, once the nuclear bomb was detonated, a series of chemical reactions would occur that would devastate all life near the blast site and miles beyond.

The Blast: An Unimaginable Power

The detonation of the nuclear weapon would release a tremendous amount of energy— about 300 trillion calories would be exerted in a fraction of a second. Most of this energy would be in the form of an intense light that atmospheric scientist Richard P. Turco describes as "a bit of sunlight brought down to Earth."[57] Amazingly, the emitted light would be approximately 5,000 times brighter than a desert sun at high noon. Indeed, the light was so intense during the bombing of the Japanese city of Hiroshima that photographs taken afterward revealed outlines that were created when flashes of heat rays instantly incinerated a person, leaving a haunting flash shadow of where they had stood or sat.

The light would immediately react with the air surrounding the explosion to create a fireball of enormous heat and power. According to nuclear weapons expert Lynn Eden, the center of this fireball would register at 200 million degrees Fahrenheit, more than four times the temperature found at the center of the sun. The fireball would then compress the area's air, forming a type of shockwave, or what scientists refer to as the blast wave. This would result in a gigantic firestorm, a powerful swirl of heat and wind that destroys everything in its path. Indeed, most of the destruction wrought by a nuclear weapon would stem from the ensuing firestorm rather than the initial blast.

A Firestorm That Would Eliminate All Life

This firestorm would consist of 750-mile-per-hour winds made of fire that would create a suction effect, pulling cars, trees, and other objects toward

> **Once the nuclear bomb was detonated, a series of chemical reactions would occur that would devastate all life near the blast site and miles beyond.**

> ## " Average air temperatures would be well above boiling; if lakes, rivers, or ponds were in the blast radius, their contents would immediately begin to bubble and evaporate. "

the center of the blast. According to the experts, the winds would cause the contents of enormous buildings to be "blown away at high speed. Window frames, glass, heavy desks, tables, filing cabinets, chairs, and other furnishings would become missiles and shrapnel."[58] Eden describes how nothing in the firestorm's path would be spared: "Light from the fireball would melt asphalt in the streets, burn paint off walls, and melt metal surfaces within a half second of the detonation. The interiors of vehicles and buildings in line of sight of the fireball would explode into flames . . . the shockwave could cause structures to cave in and might even topple large office buildings."[59] The firestorm might last between three and five hours.

Average air temperatures would be well above boiling; if lakes, rivers, or ponds were in the blast radius, their contents would immediately begin to bubble and evaporate. Not surprisingly, a blast that would make rivers boil would likely kill any living thing in the immediate vicinity. Even those who managed to get to bomb shelters might not survive. Eden speculates that

> those who sought shelter in basements of strongly constructed buildings could be poisoned by carbon monoxide seeping in, or killed by the oven-like conditions. Those who tried to escape through the streets would be incinerated by the hurricane-force winds laden with firebrands and flames. Even those able to find shelter in the lower-level sub-basements of massive buildings would likely die of eventual heat prostration, poisoning from fire-generated gases, or lack of water. The firestorm would eliminate all life in the fire zone.[60]

Finally, the explosion would generate an enormous electromagnetic pulse, called a Source Region Electro-Magnetic Pulse [SREMP] blast, which would likely incapacitate an area's communication abilities, making the catastrophe all the more confusing and chaotic. The authors of a 2006 study that simulated nuclear bombings of New York, Washington, D.C., Chicago, and Atlanta concluded that "the combination of SREMP on electronics, and blast effects on antenna integrity and alignment will severely curtail radio, cell phone and satellite communications in a post event environment."[61]

The Dead and the Wounded

All of this destruction could be caused with a 15-kiloton bomb, the same size bomb dropped on Hiroshima. However, it is likely the bomb would be more powerful: Modern nuclear weapons can average 300 kilotons. Experts estimate that a bomb of this size would decimate an area of between 12 and 65 square miles, depending on cloud coverage and atmospheric visibility, which would either slow or accelerate the firestorm. The 15-kiloton bomb dropped over Hiroshima completely destroyed about 8 square miles of city.

It is difficult to determine exactly how many people would be injured and killed by a nuclear explosion. The number of dead would be dependent on a variety of factors: the size and power of the blast; the strength of the ensuing firestorm; the radius of radiation exposure; the damage caused by falling buildings and wreckage; and more. As the authors of the study that simulated bombings over four American cities wrote,

> The number of dead would be dependent on a variety of factors: the size and power of the blast; the strength of the ensuing firestorm; the radius of radiation exposure; the damage caused by falling buildings and wreckage; and more.

Due to the combination of injury categories, death rates can be exacerbated far beyond that expected for any one of the injuries taken alone. Victims cannot move and could be consumed by fire or are simply left to die due to lack of resources. Others fall victim to poor sanitation due to failure of the main power, water and waste facilities. Lack of immediate (12 hours) or even intermediate (48 hours) health care often results in the body going into shock or succumbing to infection, which would not have occurred had basic health care been available.[62]

This study determined that a 20-kiloton bomb would kill about 1.6 million people in New York City; a 550-kiloton bomb would kill about 6.5 million. Other studies that simulated nuclear war between India and Pakistan estimate that 9 to 12 million deaths would be likely.

Radiation Fallout

In addition to instantly incinerating those within the blast site, the nuclear explosion would release large amounts of radiation into the air, which would kill and injure tens of thousands more people. Radiation is a type of energy that in small doses can be safely used for scientific purposes such as taking X-rays, but in large doses it can be very dangerous. Indeed, radiation from a nuclear blast would cause severe health problems for survivors.

> **Other victims experienced severe bleeding, burning, and skin and limb erosion as a result of exposure to radiation, in addition to high fevers, uncontrollable vomiting, and epilation (extreme hair loss).**

The land surrounding the blast would probably not stay radioactive for long if the bomb was small—according to the Radiation Effects Research Foundation, which tracks the health of Hiroshima and Nagasaki survivors, radioactivity was over 90 percent dissipated one week after the bombings and had returned to normal urban levels within one year of the explosions. But the health effects of being exposed to high levels of radiation contributed to the deaths of thousands of Japanese who survived the initial blast. "The first effects of radiation are the killing of cells and tissues. . . . Principal signs and symptoms are diarrhea from damage to the intestines, reduced blood cell counts and bleeding from damage to bone marrow, hair loss due to damaged hair-root cells, and temporary male sterility."[63] Other victims experienced severe bleeding, burning, and skin and limb erosion as a result of exposure to radiation, in addition to high fevers, uncontrollable vomiting, and epilation (extreme hair loss). Many of these victims died within days, weeks, and months of the radiation exposure.

Even those who survived the initial effects of radiation would continue to endure long-term health effects. Thousands of survivors from the Hiroshima and Nagasaki explosions experienced increased rates of cancer of all organs, disease of all organs, and abnormalities in lymph nodes and bone marrow. Furthermore, their offspring experienced higher than normal rates of stillborn death, mental retardation, and other birth defects. Although several studies have concluded that no permanent genetic mutations occurred as a result of the radiation exposure in 1945, others have pointed out that genetic mutations can take several generations to become apparent. Since radiation has been proven to cause genetic mutations in mice and other laboratory animals, some scientists believe the long-term effects of the bombings have yet to be revealed. Although the generational affects of radiation remain unclear, it is certain that if a nuclear bomb were to be exploded over a modern urban area, it would cause radiation sickness, cancer, and death in the millions.

> " The most devastating and far-reaching consequence of a nuclear war would be a dramatic alteration of Earth's average temperature. "

A Nuclear Winter

Even those who lived through the initial nuclear blast and escaped radiation poisoning would have trouble surviving, because the aftermath of the explosion could trigger such significant environmental changes that the world would be transformed into a dangerous and inhospitable place. Indeed, the most devastating and far-reaching consequence of a nuclear war would be a dramatic alteration of Earth's average temperature, heralding what Turco first referred to in the 1980s as a "nuclear winter."

A nuclear winter would be caused by enormous amounts of smoke, soot, dust, and particle refuse that followed the firestorm of a nuclear explosion. This blanket of debris would cover such large amounts of sky and be so impenetrable that the sun's rays would be blocked, cooling much of the planet. This layer would repel water, making it uneasily dissolvable, and would likely remain in the sky for at least six years. Earth would immediately begin cooling.

> Even a small nuclear war—an exchange of weapons between India and Pakistan, for example, which amount to about 0.03 percent of the world's nuclear weapons—would herald these global consequences.

Scientists estimate that on average, the temperature of the Earth's surface would drop by about 1.11°C (2°F). After 10 years, the global temperature would still be on average 0.4°F cooler than normal. "You would have a global climate change unprecedented in human history," says scientist Alan Robock. "It would instantaneously be colder than the Little Ice Age"[64] that hit Europe in the sixteenth century. Such a cooling would have harsh environmental and agricultural consequences, including severe droughts, freezes, less rain and sun, and heavily polluted air, which would likely trigger a global famine and dire shortages of water and other critical resources.

"The Greatest Danger Since the Dawn of Man"

Robock was part of a team of scientists that in December 2006 presented these grim conclusions to the American Geophysical Conference, at which scientists argued that even a small nuclear war—an exchange of weapons between India and Pakistan, for example, which amount to about 0.03 percent of the world's nuclear weapons—would induce these global consequences. For many years military strategists and scientists had believed that a small nuclear war between two regional enemies would only spell damage for the continents on which they occurred. But modern simulations such as the one endorsed by the scientists in 2006 indicate this is not so.

Scientists now believe that a nuclear war between two nations, each with 50 small, Hiroshima-size nuclear bombs, could induce cataclysmic changes that would impact life the world over. Government officials estimate there are 33 nations with enough highly enriched uranium to engineer this supply of nuclear weapons, and it is a supply likely possessed by at least 8 of the 9 nations in the nuclear club. For these reasons, Brian Toon, an atmospheric scientist at the University of Colorado and lead author on the study, has remarked that the combination of current political instability, global nuclear proliferation, and urban population density "forms perhaps the greatest danger to the stability of human society since the dawn of man."[65]

> **The interest in averting nuclear war . . . [is] truly a global responsibility.**

Although the contemporary understanding of just how devastating an even limited nuclear war would be is dire and frightening, there is one bright lining in this nuclear cloud: that citizens of all nations on Earth—not just those that might be caught in the direct crossfire of a nuclear attack—have a vested interest in preventing nuclear conflict. If citizens in the United States could be as miserably affected by an Indian-Pakistani or a North Korean–South Korean nuclear war as citizens in neighboring countries, they have as much interest in preventing it as anyone. The interest in averting nuclear war thus becomes a truly global responsibility. As the scientists of the 2006 study concluded, "The scope and severity of the hazards identified pose a significant threat to the global community. They deserve careful analysis by governments worldwide advised by a broad section of the world scientific community, as well as widespread public debate."[66]

Primary Source Quotes*

Could the World Survive a Nuclear War?

"As remote as the possibility is, all-out nuclear war has the potential to end human life on the planet—still the true doomsday scenario."

—Linda Rothstein, Catherine Auer, and Jonas Siegel, "Rethinking Doomsday," *Bulletin of the Atomic Scientists,* November/December 2004.

Rothstein is the editor of the *Bulletin of the Atomic Scientists,* a political-scientific publication in which Auer's and Siegel's stories have appeared.

"A 10-kiloton nuclear bomb (a pipsqueak in weapons terms) is smuggled into Manhattan and explodes at Grand Central. Some 500,000 people are killed and the U.S. suffers $1 trillion in direct economic damage. That scenario . . . could be a glimpse of our future."

—Nicholas D. Kristof, "A Nuclear 9/11," *New York Times,* March 10, 2004.

Kristof is a columnist for the *New York Times* and the author of *China Wakes: The Struggle for the Soul of a Rising Power.*

* Editor's Note: While the definition of a primary source can be narrowly or broadly defined, for the purposes of Compact Research, a primary source consists of: 1) results of original research presented by an organization or researcher; 2) eyewitness accounts of events, personal experience, or work experience; 3) first-person editorials offering pundits' opinions; 4) government officials presenting political plans and/or policies; 5) representatives of organizations presenting testimony or policy.

Primary Source Quotes

❝To an increasing extent, people are congregating in the world's great urban centers, creating megacities with populations exceeding 10 million individuals. At the same time, advanced technology has designed nuclear explosives of such small size they can be easily transported in a car, small plane or boat to the heart of a city. . . . Remarkably, the estimated quantities of smoke generated by attacks totaling about one megaton of nuclear explosives could lead to significant global climate perturbations.**❞**

—O.B. Toon, R.P. Turco, A. Robock, C. Bardeen, L. Oman, G.L. Stenchikov, "Atmospheric Effects and Societal Consequences of Regional Scale Nuclear Conflicts and Acts of Individual Nuclear Terrorism," Atmos. Chem. Phys. Discuss., 6, 2006.

Toon, Turco, and Robock are the lead authors on the groundbreaking study that found that even a limited nuclear war could change Earth's temperature and create grave consequences for everyone on the planet. Toon hails from the University of Colorado at Boulder; Turco from the University of California at Los Angeles; and Robock from Rutgers University. Turco was the first person to coin the term "nuclear winter" in the 1980s.

❝I think the effects of the smoke [in the 2006 study on whether a small nuclear war would induce a nuclear winter] are exaggerated, but it does give people pause to think about. It suggests that anyone who is contemplating attacking another country is not going to be immune to the impacts on their own countries.**❞**

—Steve Ghan, in Alicia Chang, "Scientists Say Even a Regional Nuclear War Could Do Severe Environmental Damage," *Santa Fe New Mexican,* December 11, 2006.

Ghan is an atmospheric scientist at the Pacific Northwest National Laboratory.

❝The fire burns so hot that the asphalt in the streets begins to melt and then burn, even as people are trying to run across it, literally melting into the pavement themselves as they run. Victims, on fire, jump into rivers, only to catch fire again when they surface for air.... For the survivors of the initial blast who do not then die in the firestorm that follows, many will die painfully over the next few weeks [as the] body is starting to break down internally, at the molecular level. The insides of those who get a severe dose of gamma radiation, but manage to survive the other traumas, whose organs had once been well defined as lungs, liver, heart, intestines, etc., begin to resemble an undefined mass of bloody pulp.❞

—Russell D. Hoffman, "The Effects of a Nuclear War," *Information Clearing House,* August 8, 2003.

Hoffman is a volunteer with the Global Energy Network Institute in San Diego and a contributor to *Information Clearing House.com*, a comprehensive Web site that presents a treasure trove of news articles and editorials.

❝Radiation exposure could lead to a variety of symptoms such as nausea, bloody diarrhea, and hemorrhages within a few days (other consequences of radiation could appear years later). These health effects are often fatal and include leukemia, thyroid cancer, breast cancer, and lung cancer, as well as non-fatal diseases such as birth defects, cataracts, mental retardation in young children, keloids, and others.❞

—Matthew McKinzie, Zia Mian, M. V. Ramana, and A.H. Nayyar, "Nuclear War in South Asia," *Foreign Policy in Focus,* June 2002.

McKinzie is a project scientist at the Natural Resources Defense Council, Mian and Ramana are researchers with the Program for Science and Global Security at Princeton University, and Nayyar is an associate professor of physics at Quaid-i-Azam University in Islamabad, Pakistan.

> **"It is certainly a good thing for the world that Hitler's crowd or Stalin's did not discover this atomic bomb. It seems to be the most terrible thing ever discovered, but it can be made the most useful."**

—Harry S. Truman, "Pages from President Harry Truman's Diary, July 17, 18, and 25, 1945," Truman Presidential Library.

Truman was the 33rd president of the United States. He made the decision to drop atomic bombs on Hiroshima and Nagasaki because he believed it was necessary to end World War II.

> **"Everything collapsed for as far as I could see. I felt the city of Hiroshima had disappeared all of a sudden. Then I looked at myself and found my clothes had turned into rags due to the heat. . . . I saw a man whose skin was completely peeled off the upper half of his body and a woman whose eye balls were sticking out. Her whole body was bleeding. A mother and her baby were lying with a skin completely peeled off."**

—Akihiro Takahashi, testimony, *Voice of Hibakusha,* National Science Foundation, 2006.

Takahashi survived the atomic bombing of the Japanese city of Hiroshima on August 6, 1945.

> **"Anything that you can do to discourage people from thinking that there is any way to win anything with a nuclear exchange is a good idea. You still have to be mega-insane to think there is any political objective for which a nuclear explosion is going to do you any good."**

—Stephen Schneider, in Brian D. Lee, "Climate Scientist Stephen Schneider Describes Chilling Consequences of a Nuclear War," *Stanford Report,* January 10, 2007.

Schneider is a climatologist at Stanford University and a senior fellow at the Woods Institute for the Environment.

Could the World Survive a Nuclear War?

- According to the **Federation of American Scientists**, the energy of a nuclear explosion is transferred to the surrounding area in three ways: first, through a blast; second, through thermal radiation; and third, through nuclear radiation. For a medium-sized weapon, the energy is distributed roughly as follows:
  - **50 percent** as blast;
  - **35 percent** as thermal radiation;
  - **15 percent** as nuclear radiation; including **5 percent** as initial ionizing radiation consisting chiefly of neutrons and gamma rays emitted within the first minute after detonation, and **10 percent** as residual nuclear radiation. Residual nuclear radiation is the hazard in fallout.

- According to a 2006 report by atmospheric scientists:
  - Earth's climate could be severely altered by explosions using less than **0.1 percent** of the world's nuclear weapons.
  - Such a war could produce fatalities comparable to all of those worldwide in World War II, which claimed approximately **72 million lives**.
  - If a **Hiroshima-size nuclear weapon** were exploded over an average city, the following nations would suffer the following injuries and casualties:
    - **Argentina**: 300,000 wounded, 526,000 dead
    - **Brazil**: 362,000 wounded, 746,000 dead
    - **China**: 562,000 wounded, 1.3 million dead

- **Egypt**: 767,000 wounded, 1.37 million dead
- **France**: 292,000 wounded, 561,000 dead
- **India**: 576,000 wounded, 1.14 million dead
- **Iran**: 284,000 wounded, 571,000 dead
- **Israel**: 172,000 wounded, 397,000 dead
- **Japan**: 280,000 wounded, 503,000 dead
- **Pakistan**: 653,000 wounded, 1.15 million dead
- **Russia**: 386,000 wounded, 685,000 dead
- **UK**: 89,000 wounded, 214,000 dead
- **United States**: 225,000 wounded, 430,000 dead

Isolated Nuclear Exchange to Cause Severe Climate Change

Scientists expect that a limited nuclear war involving less than 0.1 percent of the world's nuclear weapons would cause cataclysmic climate change. On average, the temperature of the Earth's surface would drop by 1.25 degrees Celsius, plunging all continents into climate upheaval that would lead to severe famine and drought.

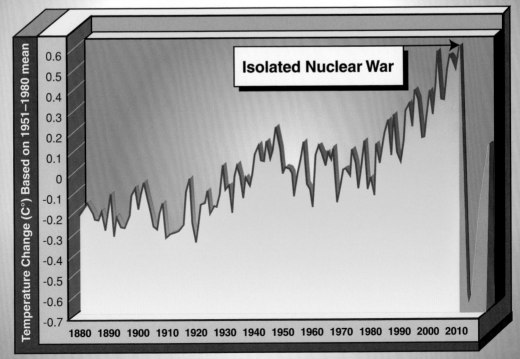

Isolated Nuclear War

Temperature Change (C°) Based on 1951–1980 mean

Source: Atmospheric Chemistry and Physics Discussions, "Climatic Consequences of Regional Nuclear Conflicts," Alan Robock et al., and NASA/Goddard Institute for Space Studies, 2006.

Climate Impact of an Isolated Nuclear War

A simulated nuclear explosion revealed that a small nuclear war would likely cover the planet in debris, lowering the average global temperature more than 2.25 degrees Fahrenheit.

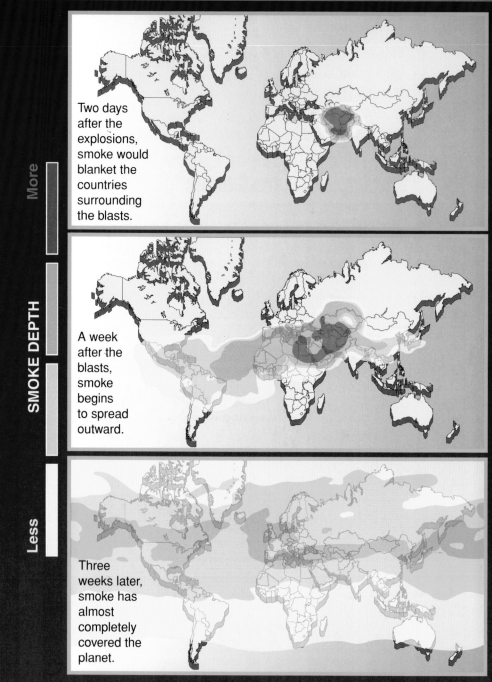

More

SMOKE DEPTH

Less

Two days after the explosions, smoke would blanket the countries surrounding the blasts.

A week after the blasts, smoke begins to spread outward.

Three weeks later, smoke has almost completely covered the planet.

Source: Atmospheric Chemistry and Physics Discussions, "Climatic Consequences of Regional Nuclear Conflicts," by Alan Robock, 2006.

Radiation Exposure

Radiation in small doses, such as the occasional X-ray, is safe for human beings. But large doses, such as those from a nuclear explosion, can cause extreme sickness, disease, and death. This illustration shows the decreasing impact of exposure to radiation as the distance from the bomb site increases.

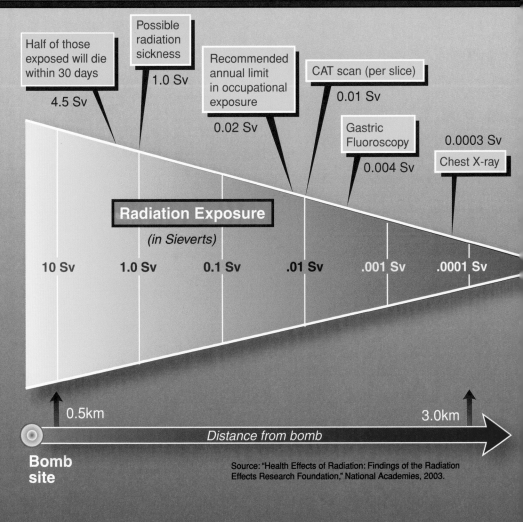

Half of those exposed will die within 30 days
4.5 Sv

Possible radiation sickness
1.0 Sv

Recommended annual limit in occupational exposure
0.02 Sv

CAT scan (per slice)
0.01 Sv

Gastric Fluoroscopy
0.004 Sv

0.0003 Sv
Chest X-ray

Radiation Exposure
(in Sieverts)

10 Sv   1.0 Sv   0.1 Sv   .01 Sv   .001 Sv   .0001 Sv

0.5km   3.0km

Distance from bomb

Bomb site

Source: "Health Effects of Radiation: Findings of the Radiation Effects Research Foundation," National Academies, 2003.

Casualties from a Small Nuclear Strike

Scientists estimate that a small nuclear strike would cause millions of deaths if detonated in the following urban areas.

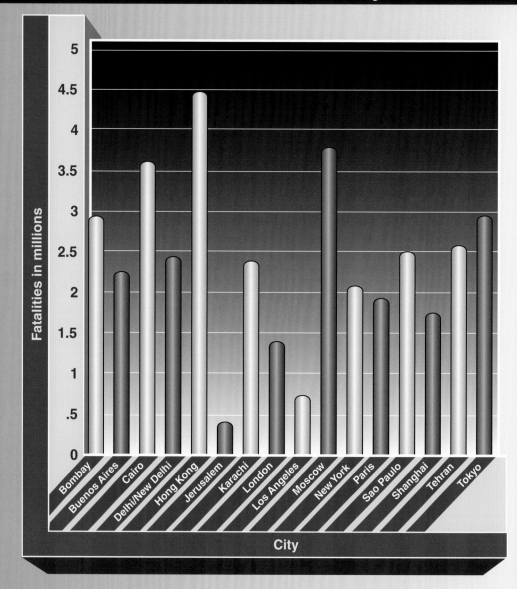

Source: "Atmospheric Effects and Societal Consequences of Regional Scale Nuclear Conflicts and Acts of Individual Nuclear Terror," O. B. Toon. Atmospheric Chemistry and Physics Discussions, 6, 2006, p. 11,747–11,748. www.copernicus.org.

- According to a 2006 study by University of Georgia scientists that **simulated nuclear explosions** over four American cities:
  - A 20-kiloton bomb would cause
    - **188,430** deaths in Washington, D.C.
    - **1,649,587** deaths in New York City
    - **614,535** deaths in Chicago
    - **182,717** deaths in Atlanta
  - A 550-kiloton bomb would cause
    - **6,456,056** deaths in New York City
    - **2,678,638** deaths in Washington, D.C.
    - **3,398,527** deaths in Chicago
    - **1,243,165** deaths in Atlanta

- The city of Hiroshima, Japan, was destroyed on August 6, 1945, by a nuclear weapon code-named "Little Boy." It is estimated that as many as **140,000 people** were killed in Hiroshima by the bomb and its aftermath.

- The city of Nagasaki, Japan, was destroyed on August 9, 1945, by a nuclear weapon code-named "Fat Man." It is estimated that as many as **74,000 people** were killed in Nagasaki by the bomb and its aftermath.

Key People and Advocacy Groups

Mahmoud Ahmadinejad: President of the Islamic Republic of Iran, Ahmadinejad insists that Iran's nuclear program is for peaceful purposes only and has refused to dismantle it despite the demands of the United Nations.

George W. Bush: Bush is America's 43rd president. Following the September 11 terrorist attacks, Bush withdrew from the 1972 Antiballistic Missile Treaty that prohibited the United States and Russia from testing and deploying ballistic missile defense systems. Bush also launched the war against Iraq to prevent dictator Saddam Hussein from developing weapons of mass destruction.

Albert Einstein: Regarded as one of the greatest scientists of all time, in 1939 Einstein and a colleague wrote a letter to President Franklin Delano Roosevelt urging the United States to develop nuclear weapons before the Nazis did. His insights led to the formation of the Manhattan Project. Einstein later expressed regret over his role in the development of the atom bomb and focused his efforts on trying to stop nuclear testing and the invention of more powerful nuclear weapons. Before he died, Einstein signed the Russell-Einstein Manifesto, which led to the creation of the Pugwash Conferences on Science and World Affairs, an international organization that seeks to reduce armed conflict.

The Federation of American Scientists (FAS): FAS is a nonprofit group created in 1945 by scientists who worked on the Manhattan Project. FAS believes that scientists, engineers, and technological inventors have an ethical obligation to use their scientific knowledge to inform political decisions. Their initial projects were devoted to controlling the spread and use of nuclear weapons, and they continue to work toward nuclear obsolescence and prevention of plutonium and highly enriched uranium reprocessing projects.

A.Q. Khan: Khan is known as the father of Pakistan's nuclear weapons program. In 2004, he confessed to heading a clandestine international network of nuclear weapons technology proliferation in which he shared Pakistan's nuclear secrets with Libya, Iran, and North Korea.

Kim Jong Il: Kim Jong Il is the dictator of North Korea. After decades of being at odds with the international community over its nuclear weapons program, North Korea successfully developed a nuclear weapon and tested it on October 6, 2006.

Richard G. Lugar: A Republican U.S. senator from Indiana since 1976, Lugar was a cosponsor of the Nunn-Lugar Cooperative Threat Reduction Program, which provides money to safeguard old Soviet nuclear weapons stocks and to employ former nuclear weapons scientists.

The Manhattan Project: The U.S. Army Corps of Engineers' Manhattan Project took place from 1942–1946 to develop nuclear weapons during World War II. The project successfully made three nuclear weapons; a test weapon called "Trinity" that was exploded in the New Mexico desert on July 16, 1945; "Little Boy," detonated over Hiroshima on August 6; and "Fat Man," dropped over Nagasaki on August 9.

Samuel Nunn: A U.S. senator from Georgia until 1996, Nunn was a cosponsor of the Nunn-Lugar Cooperative Threat Reduction Program, which provides money to safeguard old Soviet nuclear weapons stocks and to employ former nuclear weapons scientists.

J. Robert Oppenheimer: The physicist in charge of the Manhattan Project, Oppenheimer is referred to as "the father of the atomic bomb." After the bombing of Hiroshima and Nagasaki at the end of World War II, Oppenheimer regretted his role in creating the most destructive weapon the world had ever seen. After the war he became an adviser to the U.S. Atomic Energy Commission and warned against escalating the nuclear arms race that developed during the Cold War.

Al Qaeda: Al Qaeda is Osama bin Laden's terrorist group. Bin Laden formed al Qaeda in the 1980s to fight Soviet soldiers in Afghanistan. Since then al Qaeda's focus has turned toward fighting the United States. Al Qaeda is interested in obtaining nuclear weapons to use in a terrorist attack.

Chronology

1905
Albert Einstein develops the theory of relativity, a formula that states that mass can be converted into energy. This theory forms the basis for the development of nuclear technologies.

1942–1946
The Manhattan Project, funded by the U.S. Army Corps of Engineers and directed by J. Robert Oppenheimer, develops three atomic bombs.

1949
The Soviet Union successfully tests an atomic bomb, becoming the world's second nuclear power.

November 1952
The United States detonates the first hydrogen bomb in the Marshall Islands. At 10.4 megatons, the explosion is nearly 700 times more powerful than the bomb exploded at Nagasaki.

1960
France becomes the world's fourth nuclear power.

1964
Communist China ac-quires nuclear weap with the help of its the Soviet Union.

May 1972
The first round of Stra gic Arms Limitation T (SALT I) ends with U. Soviet presidents signi Anti-Ballistic Missile (Treaty, which limits th ing and deployment of listic missile defense sy The ABM treaty enter force on October 3.

| 1900 | 1940 | 1945 | 1950 | 1955 | 1960 | 1965 | 1970 | 1975 |

August 1945
Atom bombs are dropped on the Japanese cities of Hiroshima and Naga-saki, killing more than 200,000 people and end-ing World War II.

1962
A 13-day standoff over nuclear weapons in Cuba brings the United States and the Soviet Union to the brink of nuclear war.

1974
India, not a signa-tory to the Nuclear Non-Proliferation Treaty, develops nuclear weapons.

1939
Einstein sends a letter to Presi-dent Franklin D. Roosevelt warn-ing him that Nazi Germany may be researching nuclear weapons. Roosevelt forms a special com-mittee to investigate the military implications of atomic research.

August 1953
The Soviet Union announces it pos-sesses the hydrogen bomb. The Cold War arms race of-ficially begins.

1968
The Nuclear Non-Prolifera-tion Treaty (NPT) is opened for signature (meaning that countries are able to sign it). The agreement allows the five states that had weapons prior to the treaty to retain their arsenals. It prevents these states from assisting any other state from developing nuclear weapons and prohib-its nonnuclear-weapons states from ever developing them.

1952
British scientists from the Manhat-tan Project help the United King-dom acquire nuclear weapons.

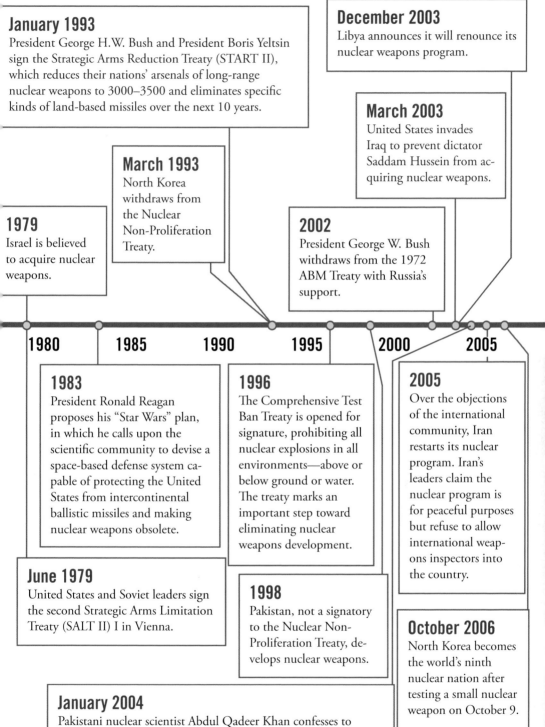

January 1993
President George H.W. Bush and President Boris Yeltsin sign the Strategic Arms Reduction Treaty (START II), which reduces their nations' arsenals of long-range nuclear weapons to 3000–3500 and eliminates specific kinds of land-based missiles over the next 10 years.

December 2003
Libya announces it will renounce its nuclear weapons program.

March 2003
United States invades Iraq to prevent dictator Saddam Hussein from acquiring nuclear weapons.

March 1993
North Korea withdraws from the Nuclear Non-Proliferation Treaty.

1979
Israel is believed to acquire nuclear weapons.

2002
President George W. Bush withdraws from the 1972 ABM Treaty with Russia's support.

1980   1985   1990   1995   2000   2005

1983
President Ronald Reagan proposes his "Star Wars" plan, in which he calls upon the scientific community to devise a space-based defense system capable of protecting the United States from intercontinental ballistic missiles and making nuclear weapons obsolete.

1996
The Comprehensive Test Ban Treaty is opened for signature, prohibiting all nuclear explosions in all environments—above or below ground or water. The treaty marks an important step toward eliminating nuclear weapons development.

2005
Over the objections of the international community, Iran restarts its nuclear program. Iran's leaders claim the nuclear program is for peaceful purposes but refuse to allow international weapons inspectors into the country.

June 1979
United States and Soviet leaders sign the second Strategic Arms Limitation Treaty (SALT II) I in Vienna.

1998
Pakistan, not a signatory to the Nuclear Non-Proliferation Treaty, develops nuclear weapons.

October 2006
North Korea becomes the world's ninth nuclear nation after testing a small nuclear weapon on October 9.

January 2004
Pakistani nuclear scientist Abdul Qadeer Khan confesses to having shared nuclear secrets with North Korea, Libya, and Iran.

Related Organizations

The American Civil Defense Association (TACDA)

11576 S. State St., Suite #502
Draper, UT 84020
phone: (800) 425-5397
e-mail: defense@tacda.org
Web site: www.tacda.org

TACDA promotes civil defense awareness and disaster preparedness, both in the military and private sector, and aims to assist citizens in their efforts to prepare for all types of natural and man-made disasters. Publications include the quarterly *Journal of Civil Defense* and the *TACDA Alert* newsletter.

America's Future

7800 Bonhomme Ave.
St. Louis, MO 63105
phone: (314) 725-6003
e-mail: info@americasfuture.net
Web site: www.americasfuture.net

America's Future supports continued U.S. testing of nuclear weapons and their usefulness as a deterrent to war. The group publishes the monthly newsletter *America's Future*.

Arms Control Association (ACA)

1150 Connecticut Ave. NW, Suite 620
Washington, DC 20036
phone: (202) 463-8270
e-mail: aca@armscontrol.org
Web site: www.armscontrol.org

The Arms Control Association believes the world should limit arms, reduce international tensions, and promote world peace. ACA publishes the monthly magazine *Arms Control Today,* which frequently features articles about nuclear weapons.

Carnegie Endowment for International Peace

1779 Massachusetts Ave. NW
Washington, DC 20036
phone: (202) 483-7600
e-mail: info@ceip.org
Web site: www.ceip.org

The Carnegie Endowment for International Peace conducts research on international affairs and U.S. foreign policy. Issues concerning nuclear weapons and proliferation are often discussed in articles published in its quarterly journal *Foreign Policy.*

Center for Defense Information (CDI)

1779 Massachusetts Ave. NW, Suite 615
Washington, DC 20036
phone: (202) 332-0600
e-mail: info@cdi.org
Web site: www.cdi.org

CDI is composed of civilians and former military officers who oppose both excessive expenditures for weapons and policies that increase the danger of war. The center monitors the military and analyzes spending, policies, weapon systems, and related military issues.

Center for Nonproliferation Studies (CNS)

460 Pierce St.
Monterey, CA 93940
phone: (831) 647-4154
e-mail: cns@miis.edu;
Web site: http://cns.miis.edu

CNS researches all aspects of nonproliferation and works to combat the spread of weapons of mass destruction. It produces research databases and has multiple reports, papers, speeches, and congressional testimony available online. Its main publication is the *Nonproliferation Review.*

Federation of American Scientists

1717 K St. NW, Suite 209
Washington, DC 20036
phone: (202) 546-3300

Web site: www.fas.org

The Federation of American Scientists was formed in 1945 by atomic scientists from the Manhattan Project who felt that scientists, engineers, and other innovators had an ethical obligation to weigh in on critical national decisions pertaining to nuclear technology.

Korean Peninsula Energy Development Organization (KEDO)
Public and External Promotion and Support Division
600 Third Ave., 12th Fl.
New York, NY 10016
phone: (212) 455-0200
Web site: www.kedo.org

KEDO is an international nonprofit organization established to carry out key provisions of the Agreed Framework, negotiated in 1994 between the United States and North Korea, in which North Korea promised to freeze its nuclear facilities development. The organization works to help North Korea build civilian nuclear reactors and to provide other energy sources to that nation.

Nuclear Age Peace Foundation
1187 Coast Village Rd., Suite 1, PMB 121
Santa Barbara, California 93108-2794
phone: (805) 965-3443
Web site: www.wagingpeace.org

The Nuclear Age Peace Foundation, a nonprofit, nonpartisan international education and advocacy organization, initiates and supports worldwide efforts to abolish nuclear weapons, to strengthen international law and institutions, to use technology responsibly, and to empower youth to create a more peaceful world.

Peace Action
1100 Wayne Ave., Suite 1020
Silver Spring, MD 20910
phone: (301) 565-4050
e-mail: paprog@igc.org
Web site: www.peace-action.org

Peace Action is a grassroots peace and justice organization that works for policy changes on topics related to peace and disarmament issues. The organization produces a quarterly newsletter and also publishes an annual voting record for members of Congress.

Project Ploughshares

57 Erb St. West
Waterloo, ON, Canada N2L 6C2
phone: (519) 888-6541
e-mail: plough@ploughshares.ca
Web site: www.ploughshares.ca

Project Ploughshares promotes disarmament and demilitarization, the peaceful resolution of political conflict, and the pursuit of security based on equity, justice, and a sustainable environment.

Union of Concerned Scientists (UCS)

2 Brattle Sq.
Cambridge, MA 02238
phone: (617) 547-5552
fax: (617) 864-9405
e-mail: ucs@ucsusa.org
Web site: www.ucsusa.org

UCS is concerned about the impact of advanced technology on society. It supports nuclear arms control as a means to reduce nuclear weapons. Publications include the quarterly *Nucleus* newsletter and reports and briefs concerning nuclear proliferation.

United States Arms Control and Disarmament Agency (ACDA)

320 21st St. NW
Washington, DC 20451
phone: (800) 581-ACDA
Web site: http://dosfan.lib.uic.edu

The mission of the ACDA is to strengthen the national security of the United States by formulating, advocating, negotiating, implementing, and verifying effective arms control, nonproliferation, and disarmament policies, strategies, and agreements. The agency publishes fact sheets on the disarmament of weapons of mass destruction as well as online records of speeches, treaties, and reports related to arms control.

For Further Research

Books

Kaveh L. Afrasiabi, *Iran's Nuclear Program: Debating Facts Versus Fiction.* Charleston, SC: BookSurge, 2006.

Kurt M. Campbell, Robert J. Einhorn, Mitchell B. Reiss, eds., *The Nuclear Tipping Point: Why States Reconsider Their Nuclear Choices.* Washington, DC: Brookings Institution, 2004.

Victor D. Cha and David C. Kang, *Nuclear North Korea: A Debate on Engagement Strategies.* New York: Columbia University Press, 2005.

Gordon G. Chang, *Nuclear Showdown: North Korea Takes On the World.* New York: Random House, 2006.

Michael D. Evans and Jerome R. Corsi, *Showdown with Nuclear Iran: Radical Islam's Messianic Mission to Destroy Israel and Cripple the United States.* Nashville, TN: Nelson Current, 2006.

Mark Hitchcock, *Iran: The Coming Crisis: Radical Islam, Oil, and the Nuclear Threat.* Sisters, OR: Multnomah, 2006.

Bradley K. Martin, *Under the Loving Care of the Fatherly Leader: North Korea and the Kim Dynasty.* New York: Thomas Dunne, 2004.

Gavan McCormack, *Target North Korea: Pushing North Korea to the Brink of Nuclear Catastrophe.* New York: Nation, 2004.

Michael O'Hanlon and Mike M. Mochizuki, *Crisis on the Korean Peninsula: How to Deal with a Nuclear North Korea.* New York: McGraw-Hill, 2003.

Barry R. Schneider, ed., *Avoiding the Abyss: Progress, Shortfalls, and the Way Ahead in Combating the WMD Threat.* Westport, CT: Praeger Security International, 2006.

Kenneth R. Timmerman, *Countdown to Crisis: The Coming Nuclear Showdown with Iran.* New York: Crown, 2006.

James D. Torr, *Responding to Attack: The Firefighters and the Police.* The Lucent Library of Homeland Security. San Diego: Lucent, 2003.

Al Venter, *Iran's Nuclear Option: Tehran's Quest for the Atom Bomb.* Drexel Hill, PA: Casemate, 2005.

Norbert Vollertsen, *Inside North Korea.* New York: Encounter, 2006.

Periodicals

Steve Andreasen and Dennis Gormley, "Edging Ever Closer to a Nuclear Death," *Minneapolis Star Tribune,* March 29, 2006.

William M. Arkin, "The Continuing Misuses of Fear," *Bulletin of the Atomic Scientists,* vol. 62, no. 5, September/October 2006.

Reza Aslan, "Misunderstanding Iran," *Nation,* February 28, 2005.

Gawdat Bahgat, "Nonproliferation Success: The Libyan Model," *World Affairs,* Summer 2005.

Doug Bandow, "The Hunger Artist: Starvation and Nuclear Extortion Are Kim Jong Il's Weapons of Choice," *Weekly Standard,* October 10, 2005.

Dorothy Boulware, "Is the USA Ready for War at Home?" *Afro-American,* July 29–August 4, 2006.

William F. Buckley Jr., "Presidential Dilemmas," *National Review,* December 5, 2005.

George Bunn, "Enforcing International Standards: Protecting Nuclear Materials from Terrorists Post-9/11," *Arms Control Today,* January/ February 2007.

George W. Bush, "Remarks by the President on Weapons of Mass Destruction Proliferation," February 11, 2004. www.whitehouse.gov.

Ted Galen Carpenter, "Iran's Nuclear Program, America's Policy Options," Cato Institute, *Policy Analysis,* no. 578, September 20, 2006.

David Cortright, "The New Nuclear Danger: A Strategy of Selective Coercion Is Fundamentally Flawed," *America,* December 11, 2006.

Daniel Doron, "Yes, Iran Can Be Stopped," *Weekly Standard,* February 1, 2007.

Michael Duffy, "What Would War Look Like?" *Time,* September 25, 2006.

Gwynne Dyer, "Why Not Offer Kim Jong-Il Something of Value to Head Off a Nuclear Crisis?" *Athens (OH) News,* October 12, 2006.

Economist, "Bend Them, Break Them; America and a Nuclear India," October 22, 2005.

——"Going Critical, Defying the World," October 21, 2006.

M.M. Eskandari-Qajar, "All Talk, No Nukes," *Santa Barbara (CA) Independent*, January 26–February 2, 2006.

Trevor Findlay, "Why Treaties Work or Don't Work," *Behind the Headlines,* Autumn 2005.

Robert L. Gallucci, "Let's Make a Deal," *Time,* October 23, 2006.

Dennis M. Gormley, "Securing Nuclear Obsolescence," *Survival,* Autumn 2006.

Han Sung-Joo, "Better than Nothing," *Time International,* February 26, 2007.

Robert E. Hunter, "The Iran Case: Addressing Why Countries Want Nuclear Weapons," *Arms Control Today,* December 2004.

Liaquat Ali Khan, "Nuclear Non-Proliferation Treaty Poised to Fall Apart," *Counterpunch,* May 4, 2005. www.counterpunch.org.

Nicholas D. Kristof, "Send in the Fat Guys," *New York Times,* October 22, 2006.

William Kristol, "And Now Iran: We Can't Rule Out the Use of Military Force," *Weekly Standard,* January 23, 2006.

William Langewiesche, "Living with the Bomb," *Los Angeles Times,* October 15, 2006.

Anatol Lieven and John Hulsman, "North Korea's Not Our Problem," *Los Angeles Times,* October 11, 2006.

Angie C. Marek, "A Nuclear Headache," *U.S. News & World Report,* February 26, 2007.

Judith Miller, "Gadhafi's Leap of Faith," *Wall Street Journal,* May 17, 2006.

Stephen G. Rademaker, U.S. statement at the 2005 Nuclear Non-Proliferation Treaty Review Conference, May 2, 2005. www.state.gov.

Susan E. Rice, "We Need to Talk to North Korea," *Washington Post,* June 3, 2005.

Pandy R. Sinish and Joel A. Vilensky, "WMDs in Our Backyards," *Earth Island Journal,* Winter 2005.

Fareed Zakaria, "Let Them Eat Carrots," *Newsweek,* October 23, 2006.

Stephen Zunes, "The Iranian Nuclear Threat: Myth and Reality," *Tikkun,* January/February 2007.

Web Sites

Center for Biosecurity of the University of Pittsburgh Medical Center (www.upmc-biosecurity.org).

The Center for Nonproliferation Studies (www.cns.miis.edu).

Downwinders (www.downwinders.org).

Federation of American Scientists (www.fas.org).

The Non-Proliferation Project (www.carnegieendowment.org/npp).

Public Health Emergency Preparedness and Response (www.bt.cdc.gov).

Source Notes

Overview

1. Treaty on the Non-Proliferation of Nuclear Weapons, Articles I and II, July 1, 1968. www.fas.org.
2. Stephen G. Rademaker, "U.S. Statement at the 2005 Nuclear Non-Proliferation Treaty Review Conference," May 2, 2005. www.state.gov.
3. Liaquat Ali Khan, "On the Brink: Nuclear Non-Proliferation Treaty Poised to Fall Apart," Counterpunch, May 4, 2005. www.counterpunch.org.
4. Gwynne Dyer, "Why Not Offer Kim Jong-Il Something of Value to Head Off a Nuclear Crisis?" *Athens (OH) News,* October 12, 2006.
5. Robert L. Gallucci, "Let's Make a Deal," *Time,* October 23, 2006, p. 38.
6. Ilan Berman, "Nuclear Capabilities of Iran," statement before the Senate Committee on Homeland Security and Governmental Affairs, Subcommittee on Federal Financial Management, Government Information, and International Security, November 15, 2005.
7. Robert E. Hunter, "What Happens If Iran Gets 'The Bomb'?" *Arms Control Today,* December 2004, p. 22.
8. Stephen Zunes, "The Iranian Nuclear Threat: Myth and Reality," *Tikkun,* January/February 2007, p. 29.
9. Khan, "On the Brink."
10. Dyer, "Why Not Offer Kim Jong-Il Something of Value?"
11. Dyer, "Why Not Offer Kim Jong-Il Something of Value?"
12. David C. Kang and Aaron L. Friedberg, "How to Control a Nuclear North Korea?" Council on Foreign Relations, December 6, 2006. www.cfr.org.
13. Ted Galen Carpenter, "Iran's Nuclear Program: America's Policy Options," Cato Institute *Policy Analysis,* no. 578, September 20, 2006. www.cato.org.
14. Zunes, "The Iranian Nuclear Threat: Myth and Reality," p. 29.
15. Simon Jenkins, "Accept North Korea into the Nuclear Club or Bomb It Now," *Guardian* (Manchester), October 11, 2006. www.guardian.co.uk.
16. John F. Kennedy, "The President's News Conference of March 21st, 1963," American Presidency Project. www.presidency.ucsb.edu.
17. William M. Arkin, "The Continuing Misuses of Fear," *Bulletin of the Atomic Scientists,* vol. 62, no. 5, September/October 2006, pp. 42–45.
18. David Cortright, "The New Nuclear Danger: A Strategy of Selective Coercion Is Fundamentally Flawed," *America,* December 11, 2006.
19. William Langewiesche, "Living with the Bomb; North Korea Won't Be the Last Country to Go Nuclear. Get Used to It," *Los Angeles Times,* October 15, 2006, p. M1.
20. Jenkins, "Accept North Korea into the Nuclear Club."

Is the United States Likely to Be Attacked with Nuclear Weapons?

21. Osama bin Laden, statement, trans. PBS, *Online NewsHour,* PBS.org, October 7, 2001. www.pbs.org.
22. Quoted in Graham Allison, "How to Stop Nuclear Terror," *Foreign Affairs,* January /February 2004, p. 64.
23. George Tenet, "Written Statement for the Record of the Director of Central Intelligence Before the National

Commission on Terrorist Attacks upon the United States," March 24, 2002, p. 32.

24. Patrick Briley, "Hezbollah, WMD Attacks, Inside U.S. Cities?" NewsWith Views.com, February 10, 2006.

25. Allison, "How to Stop Nuclear Terror," p. 64.

26. Linda Rothstein, Catherine Auer, and Jonas Siegel, "Rethinking Doomsday: Loose Nukes, Nanobots, Smallpox, Oh My! In This Age of Endless Imagining, and Some Very Real Risks, Which Terrorist Threats Should Be Taken Most Seriously?" *Bulletin of the Atomic Scientists,* November/December 2004, pp. 36–47.

27. *Detroit News,* "9/11: Five Years Later, Are We Safe Enough? Reluctance to Confront Radicals Leaves U.S. Vulnerable," September 11, 2006, p. A6.

28. Carpenter, "Iran's Nuclear Program: America's Policy Options."

29. Langewiesche, "Living with the Bomb," p. M1.

30. Arkin, "The Continuing Misuses of Fear," pp. 42–45.

31. <missing: Allison, p. 24>

32. John R. Bolton, statement to the 2004 Nuclear Suppliers Group Plenary Meeting, Göteborg, Sweden, May 27, 2004. www.state.gov.

33. Cristina Chuen, "Reducing the Risk of Nuclear Terrorism: Decreasing the Availability of HEU," Center for Nonproliferation Studies, May 6, 2005. http://cns.miis.edu.

34. Rothstein, Auer, and Siegel, "Rethinking Doomsday," pp. 36–47.

How Can the Spread of Nuclear Weapons Be Prevented?

35. George W. Bush, "Remarks by the President on National Missile Defense," December 12, 2001. www. whitehouse.gov.

36. Steve Andreasen and Dennis Gormley, "Edging Ever Closer to a Nuclear Death," *Minneapolis Star Tribune,* March 29, 2006.

37. Richard G. Lugar, address to the UN Security Council, February 6, 2006. http://lugar.senate.gov.

38. Linton Brooks, "Cooperative Nonproliferation and U.S.-Russian Cooperation," comments, Moscow State Institute of International Relations, May 22, 2003. www.nnsa.doe.gov.

39. George W. Bush, "Remarks by the President on Weapons of Mass Destruction Proliferation," February 11, 2004. www.whitehouse.gov.

40. Galluci, "Let's Make a Deal," p. 38.

41. Susan E. Rice, "We Need to Talk to North Korea," *Washington Post,* June 3, 2005, p. A23.

42. Anatol Lieven and John Hulsman, "North Korea Isn't Our Problem," *Los Angeles Times,* October 11, 2006.

43. Quoted in Judy Aita, "Security Council Imposes Sanctions on North Korea," U.S. Department of State, October 14, 2006. http://usinfo.state.gov.

44. Nicholas D. Kristof, "Send in the Fat Guys," *New York Times,* October 22, 2006, p. 4.

45. Ted Galen Carpenter and Christopher Preble, "North Korean Sanctions: A Cruel Mirage," Cato Institute, November 13, 2006. www.cato.org.

46. M.M. Eskandari-Qajar, "All Talk, No Nukes," *Santa Barbara (CA) Independent,* vol. 20, no. 2, January 26–February 2, 2006, p. 11.

47. William Kristol, "And Now Iran; We Can't Rule Out the Use of Military Force," *Weekly Standard,* January 23, 2006.

How Can the United States Defend Itself Against a Nuclear Attack?

48. Roger Allan, "Homeland Security's Techno War on Terror: Technologies

Combine to Detect Radiological, Biological, and Chemical Weapons of Mass Destruction," *Electronic Design*, June 29, 2006.

49. Eric Lipton, "Testers Slip Radioactive Materials over Borders," *New York Times,* March 28, 2006. www.nytimes.com.

50. Quoted in Spencer S. Hsu, "U.S. Weighs How Best to Defend Against Nuclear Threats: Proven Technology vs. New Advances," *Washington Post,* April 15, 2006, p. A3

51. Quoted in Rupert Cornwell, "Real Star Wars: Bush Revives Missile Defense Plan," Commondreams.org, May 30, 2005. www.commondreams.org.

52. U.S. Nuclear Regulatory Commission, "Consideration of Potassium Iodide in Emergency Planning," February 27, 2007. www.nrc.gov.

53. Quoted in National Institutes of Health, "NIAID Awards $4 Million to Develop Anti-Radiation Treatments," September 25, 2006. www3.niaid.nih.gov.

54. Quoted in Sam Fahmy, "Study Details Catastrophic Impact of Nuclear Attack on US Cities," University of Georgia Public Affairs Bureau, March 20, 2007. www.uga.edu.

55. William C. Bell and Cham E. Dallas, "Vulnerability of Populations and the Urban Health Care Systems to Nuclear Weapon Attack—Examples from Four American Cities," *International Journal of Health Geographics,* Center for Mass Destruction Defense, University of Georgia, February 28, 2007. www.ij-healthgeographics.com.

56. Bell and Dallas, "Vulnerability of Populations."

Could the World Survive a Nuclear War?

57. Quoted in Sid Perkins, "Sudden Chill: Even a Limited Nuclear Exchange Could Trigger a Climate Catastrophe," *Science News,* February 3, 2007, p. 74.

58. Lynn Eden, "City on Fire," *Bulletin of the Atomic Scientists,* January/February 2004.

59. Eden, "City on Fire."

60. Eden, "City on Fire."

61. Bell and Dallas, "Vulnerability of Populations."

62. Bell and Dallas, "Vulnerability of Populations."

63. Radiation Effects Research Foundation (RERF), "Health Effects of Radiation," National Academies, 2003. http://dels.nas.edu.

64. Quoted in *ABCNews.com*, "Even a Small Nuclear War Could Change the World," December 12, 2006. http://abcnews.go.com.

65. Quoted in Perkins, "Sudden Chill."

66. O.B. Toon, R.P. Turco, A. Robock, C. Bardeen, L. Oman, G.L. Stenchikov, "Atmospheric Effects and Societal Consequences of Regional Scale Nuclear Conflicts and Acts of Individual Nuclear Terrorism," Atmos. Chem. Phys. Discuss., 6, 2006, pp. 11747–11748. www.copernicus.org.

List of Illustrations

List of Illustrations

Index

About the Author

Lauri S. Friedman earned her bachelor's degree in religion and political science from Vassar College. Her studies there focused on political Islam, and she produced a thesis on the Islamic revolution in Iran titled "Neither West, nor East, but Islam." She also holds a preparatory degree in flute performance from the Manhattan School of Music.

Her other publications for ReferencePoint Press include *Compact Research: The Death Penalty* and *Compact Research: Terrorist Attacks*. She has also edited numerous publications for Greenhaven Press on controversial social issues such as gay marriage, Islam, terrorism, racism, assisted suicide, the Middle East, prisons, the Internet, and the Patriot Act.

Lauri lives near the beach in San Diego with her partner Randy and their yellow lab, Trucker. In her spare time she enjoys pottery, making music, and traveling.